USING MICROSOFT ACCESS

A How-To-Do-It Manual for Librarians

E. Sonny Butler, Ph.D.

HOW-TO-DO-IT MANUALS
FOR LIBRARIANS

NUMBER 76

NEAL-SCHUMAN PUBLISHERS, INC.
New York, London

3.13.01

Published by Neal-Schuman Publishers, Inc.
100 Varick Street
New York, NY 10013

Copyright © 1997 by E. Sonny Butler, Ph.D.

All rights reserved. Reproduction of this book, in whole or in part, without
written permission of the publisher, is prohibited.

Printed and bound in the United States of America.

Library of Congress Cataloging-in-Publication Data

Butler, E. Sonny.
　Using Microsoft Access : how-to-do-it manual / E. Sonny Butler.
　　p.　cm.—(How-to-do-it manual for librarians ; no. 76)
　Includes index.
　ISBN 1–55570–268–6
　1. Libraries—Automation—Handbooks, manuals, etc. 2. Database
management—Computer programs—Handbooks, manuals, etc.
3. Microsoft Access—Handbooks, manuals, etc. I. Title.
II. Series: How-to-do-it manuals for libraries ; no 76.
Z699.4.M226B87　1997
025'.00285'574—dc21   97–27406
                                                           CIP

CONTENTS

FIGURES

PREFACE

Much of what librarians do today requires adeptness in creating and manipulating databases. As information specialists we need to be able not only to use various databases but also to understand and explain their underlying principles and functions. It is only by possessing both these skills and this knowledge that we can design and build databases that serve our library's needs and modify them when required.

All too often when we buy predesigned application software, we are dependent upon the vendor that wrote the original application to make changes for us. My earlier book, ***Using dBASE Version 5 for Windows™: A How-To Do It Manual for Librarians*** demonstrated how librarians could take more control of their information management using a popular database management system. This new book serves a similar function for another powerful database, Microsoft® Access for Windows. I decided to write a new manual on using Microsoft Access for Windows because more and more libraries are choosing this program because of its ability to have a seamless interface with the other Microsoft Office applications such as Word, Excel, and PowerPoint.

This manual is intended to assist librarians in designing unique applications that meet specific and sometimes unique library needs. It does this by using library specific examples and by demonstrating how Access can be used to meet those needs. The examples cover designing the database, adding entries, enhancing the structure, preparing reports, and printing.

It seems like software changes far more rapidly than we as individuals can assimilate it. This is especially true of librarians, because as information specialists we are expected to know how to use and often teach an amazingly broad array of information tools ranging from word processing programs to online catalogs to Web browsers. Most software comes with several volumes of instructions that are usually divided into user manuals, programming manuals, installation manuals, and other types of documentation. Often these manuals are several hundred pages in length, printed in small type, and several inches thick. They are so imposing you never even remove the shrink wrap to use them and anyway simple instructions such as how to get started are not to be found at the beginning of the manual.

This How-To-Do-It Manual is designed so that you can learn the fundamentals of using Microsoft Access for Windows and how the program can better assist you to manage your library's data. Then, if you need advanced instructions, it will be much easier to consult and understand a more comprehensive instruction manual because you will have mastered the fundamental concepts; thus, you will feel comfortable with Microsoft Access for Windows after using this manual.

This manual uses examples from the library profession to make it easier for the librarian to follow from chapter to chapter and topic to topic. It holds the means by which you can join the developers of specialized application software systems to meet your library's specific information management needs. This manual is current with changes to Microsoft Access for Windows through Microsoft Office Professional Version 7.

This book assumes that the reader understands the basic functions of a microcomputer system and possesses a basic understanding of the Microsoft Windows 95 operating system. As you learn to use Microsoft Access for Windows you'll apply your skills by developing applications as presented in this book and modifying them to meet your specific needs. By the end of the book you will have the knowledge necessary to develop other applications as required.

How to Use This Manual

Chapter 1 goes over the basic functions of working with Windows, describes and discusses terms such as multitasking, and shows how to use the menu and tool bars. Chapter 2 covers the basics, defines some useful terms and leads you through the steps for designing and building your first table structure. Chapter 3 deals with the data management function of database. You learn how to enter records, delete records, and find records in your overall database. Chapter 4 teaches you to sort and index data fields within your database and presents some of the advantages and disadvantages of each method. Chapter 5 introduces simple and complex queries, using operators, wild cards, and boolean logic. Chapter 6 explains the concept of relational database and how this is used in your database design and development. Chapter 7 shows how to print information from tables or queries and introduces reports and mailing labels using data from your existing tables.

Acknowledgments

I greatly appreciate the time and effort of Lawree Turner, a student at Eastern New Mexico University. I would also like to express my appreciation to both Neal-Schuman Publishers and my editor Charles Harmon for their patience, faith, and trust. I look forward to working with them in the future.

Finally, thank you for purchasing this book. I sincerely hope you will profit intellectually, personally, and professionally from the knowledge derived. Please forward your comments to the publisher and they will forward them to me for review and updates.

CHAPTER 1 WORKING WITH WINDOWS

OBJECTIVES

1.1   STARTING WINDOWS

1.2   MULTITASKING

1.3   SAVING FILES

1.4   CLOSING AND EXITING
         APPLICATIONS

Microsoft Windows 95 and Microsoft Windows 3.1 are graphical user interfaces (GUIs) that work with your application, in this case Microsoft Access, to control the basic operation of your computer. This brief overview will assist you in learning some of the basic skills you will use in Microsoft Access. We will discuss how to start Windows and how to use the mouse to start Microsoft Access in the Windows environment.

1.1 Starting Windows

Windows 95 is usually automatically started, or launched, when you turn your computer on and it boots up. Windows 3.1 is usually launched from your DOS prompt by typing "WIN" and pressing <Enter>. It becomes apparent quickly what a graphical environment looks like when you compare the Windows environment to the DOS prompt environment. As a graphical interface, Windows uses pictures and symbols, known as *icons*, to replace the many arcane commands of the DOS environment. Windows allows you to run more than one application at a time; for example, you could be using Microsoft Word, Microsoft PowerPoint, and Microsoft Access at the same time and switch between them. Running more than one application at a time is called *multitasking*.

To begin, turn on your computer. You will see some technical information on the screen while it boots. In Windows 3.1, this bootup process is directed by two files known as CONFIG.SYS and AUTOEXEC.BAT. This is about all we are going to say about these files, as they go beyond the purpose of this book. In the Windows 95 environment, CONFIG.SYS and AUTOEXEC.BAT files are replaced by files known as .INI files. Again, these files go beyond this book so I will not discuss them, but I feel it important that you know of their existence for your future use of Windows 95. When you boot Windows 95, a screen that is called your *desktop* appears. The metaphor here is an actual desktop with items placed on it. You have a **Start** button on the bottom left of your screen (you may change locations if you like, but for now let's use Windows 95 the way it installs), which I compare to the drawers in your desk. If you click on the Start button and point your mouse to **programs** you will see other files available such as Accessories, Microsoft Access, Microsoft Excel, Microsoft Word, etc.(see Figure 1.1).

From here, you may open any application by placing your mouse on that program and *clicking the left button twice*. The application will open for you to begin use.

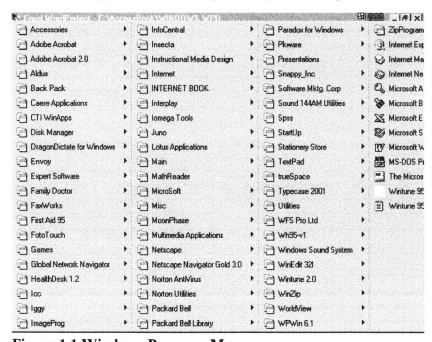

Figure 1.1 Windows Program Menu

1.2 MultiTasking

A very useful feature of the Windows environment is the ability the open multiple applications and go back and forth between them. For example, if you are doing an inventory of publications or searching a database looking for specific information, and you wish to include some of the information in MS Word, you can open both MS Word and MS Access and, by using the task bar at the bottom of the screen, switch between the applications or use another technique that involves the <ALT> and <TAB> keys. Let me explain this technique briefly. After you open all the applications you will be using, hold down the <ALT> key and press the <TAB> key. You will see a window pop up with the name of one of the applications you have opened. Holding the <ALT> key down and continuing to tap the <Tab> key will result in other applications appearing in the window in the middle of your screen. When you arrive at the application you need, release the <ALT> key, and that application will open. You may use this technique whenever you want to move between applications. Or can use the task bar at the bottom of your screen if you are using Windows 95.

1.3 Saving Files

Any documents or databases you create are stored in the computer's *random access memory* (RAM). RAM is temporary storage space that is lost when the power to the computer is turned off. To store or save a document permanently, you need to save it to a hard or floppy disk or other secondary storage device. You need to save your database files often to insure you are able to retrieve them if an accident occurs or the power to your computer is disrupted. Saving files using MS Access is discussed further in different chapters, which pertain to specific functions of building tables and using MS Access. Figure

1.2 shows you an example of what MS Access's file menu looks like.

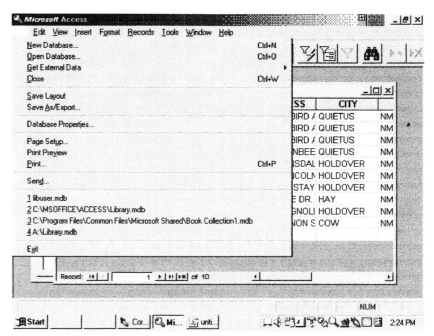

Figure 1.2 File Menu

1.4 Closing and Exiting Applications

When you have finished working with your open applications, you should save, close, and exit the application(s). If you do not save and close applications appropriately you run the risk of losing your data. Figure 1.2 illustrates the menu used for closing and exiting MS Access. When you save, close, and exit your applications, you may then exit Windows. Windows 95 has a **Shut Down** button on the Start Menu that will close any remaining open applications and prepare the computer for turning off the power.

CHAPTER 2 TABLES

OBJECTIVES

Data are a valuable resource to libraries. Libraries need to store, manipulate, and retrieve many items of information about each publication they own as well as about each registered borrower. Organizing, creating, maintaining, retrieving, and sorting such data are essential activities. One of the many tools available to accomplish these tasks is the database management system.

Most people use databases to manage their lives, although they don't name them database systems. A database is simply a collection of information, or data put together in a usable form that can be retrieved. A dictionary, card catalog, reference index, client file, or overdue list is a database. Software programs such as Microsoft Access that instruct computers how to handle data are called database management systems. As a professional librarian, you will use database technology to organize your inventory of publications, be they printed, audio, video, or any other item(s) you must maintain and account for in the library.

The most important step in designing a database is defining the problem to be addressed. Once you have defined the problem(s), you then need to decide what data you need, what kinds of data belong together in the same table, and how those tables will fit together. If you start designing the program before you have a clear idea of the solution, you have a very good chance of solving the wrong problem, just adding an unnecessary report, or leaving out something important. Changing the structure of the database is not difficult, and if you put in something unnecessary, it will not be too hard to delete all the information in those fields. However, if after you've entered a few hundred records you discover that you've left out something vital, it can be difficult and time consuming to add the field to the database structure and then enter the actual data.

In the chapters that follow, we will be developing a card catalog and a circulation record for a small, fictional library called Manchester Memorial Library. The library's users come from two separate towns with separate zip codes. We will enter information on several users and several books from the library and manipulate this information to demonstrate some of the features of Access.

When you create a database in Microsoft Access, you can use several types of files. *Tables* are the basic type of file, in which you define which data go together and enter the data in the file/table. *Queries* are files that call up certain records from the table. *Reports* are files that present the data in formatted, printed form. From now on, we will not use the term file. Instead, we will indicate which type of file we're dealing with.

The database we create will be called **LIBRARY.** The tables we will be working with in our library database are the **BOOKS** table and the **LIBUSERS** table. We will link them to form a **CHKLST** query, an **OVERDUE** query, and **SHELFLST** query. The printed reports will present the data in **NOTICE** and **LABELS**.

Many libraries get their bibliographic information from the Library of Congress or another bibliographic utility in Machine Readable Cataloging (MARC) format. The MARC format tapes provide more information than we will need for this tutorial. If you get your cataloging information from this source, you can choose which MARC tag fields you want to use. If, your library, later on, grows much larger, and you want to use more of the available cataloging information, Microsoft Access will accommodate additional fields.

Let's start thinking about the BOOKS table. Each piece of information (for instance, Author, Title, Publisher) about a book is called a field. You will need to decide the length and the data type for each field. To keep from duplicating data fields/items, you may want to create what is called a data element dictionary, in database speak, which is very analogous to a regular dictionary. You maintain all the data items along with their definitions in a file, this may be automated if you desire. As a matter of fact, you can build a manual data dictionary initially and automate it at a later date. This new data element dictionary will allow you to define all of your data fields and the characteristics of each field (such as field length), whether it contains numeric or alphabetic information, and a general description of the field for future reference. In Microsoft Access, the data types are:

- *Text.* Letters, numbers, and special characters (for example, & or #) up to 254 characters. If you choose Character as the data type, you will also have to enter a number as field width.

- *Numeric.* Holds numbers that you want to perform calculations on. Numeric fields may be up to 20 spaces wide (including decimal places).

- *Date/Time.* Holds dates or times, depending on how it is formatted, and only lets the user enter valid dates.

- *Currency.* Holds numbers used as amounts of money.

- *Counter.* Holds sequential numbers that Access automatically assigns. Access assigns the number one to the first record entered in the file, the number 2 to the second record, and so on. These numbers cannot be changed.

● *Logical.* Holds only the value T or F (or Y or N).

● *Memo.* Holds variable lengths of text. Useful for fields that might vary widely in length, or to which you need only minimum access (e.g., general notes).

● *OLE Object.* Holds data from other Windows applications that support Object Linking and Embedding. This is an advanced feature involving inserting objects from other programs, including pictures, sound, or any other type of data.

2.1 DESIGNING THE TABLE STRUCTURE

Open Microsoft Access. You should see a blank Access screen with the Title bar, Menu bar, and Speed bar at the top (see Figure 2.1).

Open

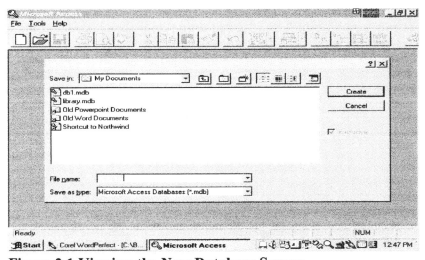

Figure 2.1 Viewing the New Database Screen

First, we will create the structure for the table **BOOKS**.

1.   Click on the **Create** button in the speed bar.
      Notice that when your mouse pointer is on the
      button, **Create a new database** appears in the
      status bar at the bottom of the screen.

2.   Type **LIBRARY** in the space labeled **File name**.
      Access will add the file extension .**mdb** where
      needed (see Figure 2.2).

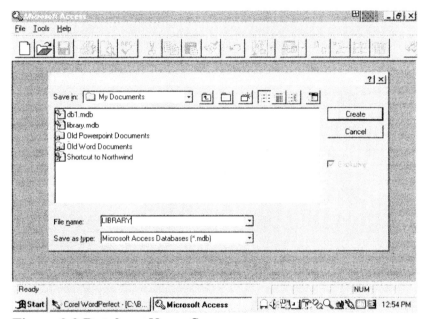

Figure 2.2 Database Name Screen

Click on **Create.** The screen you see now allows you to
define which kind of file you want to create: **Tables,
Queries, Forms, Reports, Macros, or Modules** (see
Figure 2.3).

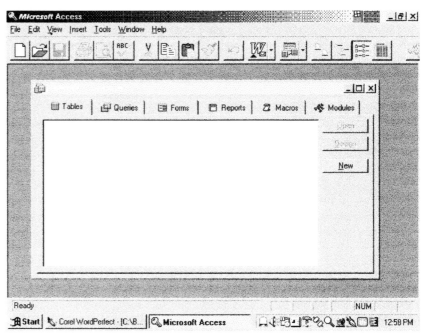

Figure 2.3 Create New Database

3.   Click **TABLE** to select it, then click **NEW**. You
        will see a screen asking you to choose between
        TABLE WIZARDS or **NEW TABLE**. Click
        NEW TABLE (see Figure 2.4).

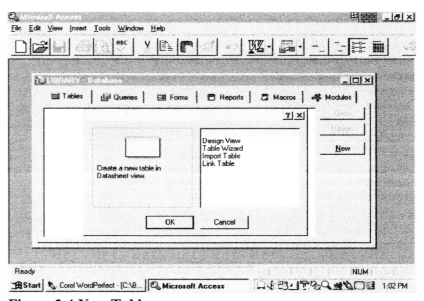

Figure 2.4 New Table

Click on **Design View**. Now you should see the screen for defining the structure of the table (see Figure 2.5).

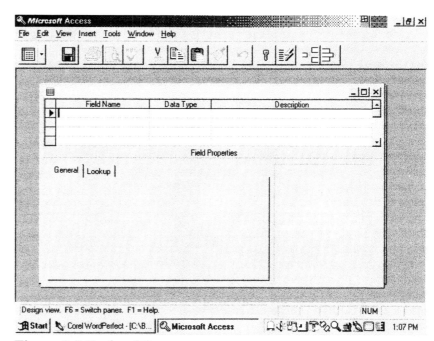

Figure 2.5 Design View

4. In the Name space for Field 1, type **AccessNo**.

5. Press **<Enter>**. The cursor moves to the **Data Type** box.

6. Click in this box to reveal an arrow at the right side of the box. Click on the arrow to reveal a drop-down box with your options for the **Data Type**. Select **Text** (which is the default choice) (see Figure 2.6).

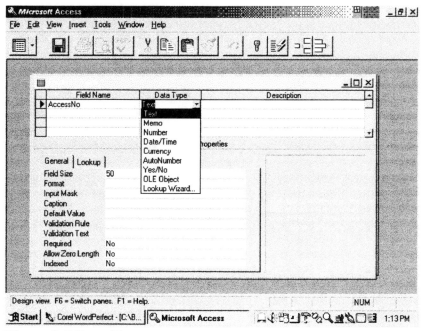

Figure 2.6 Data Type

Note: You must assign a data type for each field. The data type determines what field values you may enter for that field and what other properties the field will have. In Access, you assign one of nine data types to each field. A *drop-down box* holds a list of choices appropriate for that particular space. The space usually has a small arrowhead to indicate that there are more options. Click once on the arrow to reveal the choices and click on the one you want.

Text allows field values containing letters, digits, spaces, and special characters. Text fields may be up to 255 characters long. You should assign the text data type to fields in which you will store names, addresses, and descriptions, and to fields containing digits that are not to be used for calculations.

Memo like the text data types, allows field values containing letters, digits, spaces, and special characters. Memo fields can be up to 64,000 characters long and are used for long comments or explanations. Our application could use the memo field for storing an abstract of a publication.

Number limits field values to digits. It allows an optional leading sign to indicate a positive or negative value (+ or -) and an optional decimal point.

Date/Time allows field values containing valid dates and times only.

Currency allows field values similar to those for the Number data type.

AutoNumber consists of integers with values that are automatically inserted in the field as each new record is created. You can specify sequential numbering or random numbering. This guarantees a unique field value, so that such a field can serve as a table's primary key.

Yes/No limits field values to yes and no entries. Use this data type for fields that indicate the presence or absence of a condition, such as whether a book has been checked out.

OLE Object allows field values that are created in other software applications as objects, such as photographs, video images, graphics, drawings, sound recordings, voice mail messages, spreadsheets, and word processing documents. OLE is an acronym for object linking and embedding.

Lookup Wizard creates a field that lets you select a value from another table or from a predefined list of values.

Now that you are familiar with the various data types you can enter the appropriate type for each data field.

7.   Press <Enter> to move to the next space. This is the description box, where you can, if you like, enter a reminder to yourself of the information this field contains. For example, if you have a currency field, you may wish to remind yourself this field is an overdue fee currency field and make that notation in the description.

8.   Using either the Tab on your keyboard or the mouse, move the cursor to the Field Properties area below these boxes to further define the field.

9.   Field size determines a field value's maximum storage size for Text and Number fields. The other data types have no field size property, either because their storage size is a predetermined fixed size or because the size is dependent on the actual valued stored (e.g., a memo field).

         Maximum field size is 255.
         Default is 50; Enter 10 for AccessNo.

10.   Format allows you to specify how to display the data (e.g., (999) 999-9999).

11.   Input mask restricts data entry to the appropriate type and format required for the field. If you wish, you can create an input mask for the customer phone field that will automatically add the parentheses and hyphen to the phone number (see above). If you notice a similarity between Format and Input Mask, you are correct. Try them and see which you prefer.

12.   Click on each of these property boxes, and look at the box on the right side of the Field Properties area for hints and definitions.

Before we leave this table design, we will define the *AccessNo* field as the primary key field. This concept is used in Relational Databases, discussed fully in chapter 6. If you do not create one, Access will create a *Counter* field for you and use that as the primary key field. If you are starting a library and using Microsoft Access to catalog it from the beginning, using a Counter field is the best way to assign accession numbers. However, we are assuming that the Manchester Memorial Library already has a catalogued collection with accession numbers assigned, so we create this field.

In the rest of the fields we are defining now, leave the last three properties at the default value of **No**.

13.   Repeat steps 4-9 to define the remaining fields (see Figures 2.7, 2.8).

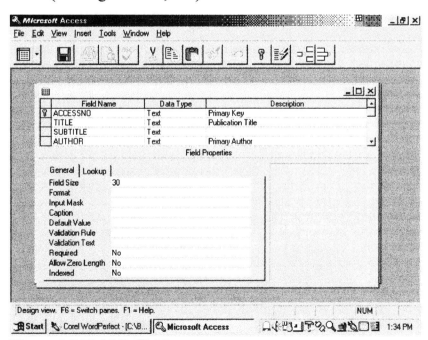

Figure 2.7 Field Definitions

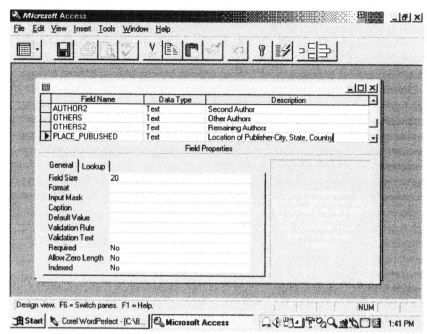

Figure 2.8 Entering Data

You will notice that the first few fields no longer appear on the screen of Access. In order to see all fields, you will need to use the scroll bars on the right side of the screen. The remainder of the database structure is listed below. See Figure 2.9 for the CHECKOUT drop down menu example.

PUBLISHER	TEXT	30
YEAR_PUBLISHED	TEXT	4
CALL_NO	TEXT	20
ISBN	TEXT	12
SUBJ_1	TEXT	50
SUBJ_2	TEXT	50
SUBJ_3	TEXT	50
CHECKOUT	YES/NO	
USER_NO	TEXT	10
DATE_DUE	DATE/TIME	
NOTES	MEMO	

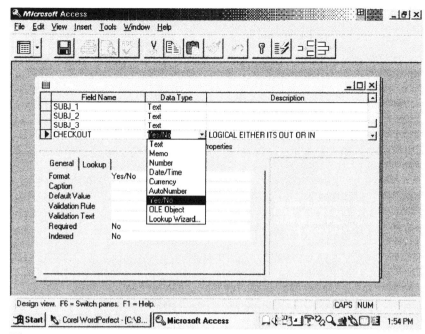

Figure 2.9 Data Type Menu

NOTE: The numbers given after the data type indicate the *Field Size* to be used in the *Field Properties* box.
In the *Checkout* field, instead of entering each date manually, simultaneously press **<Control>** and the **<Semicolon>** keys to insert today's date. Also, click on the Format box in the Field Properties and choose which date format you prefer.

Before we save this design, we need to make sure we have specified the **AccessNo** field as the primary key field.

14.   Highlight the ACCESSNO field and click on the **Primary Key** in the tool bar above the screen (see Figure 2.10).

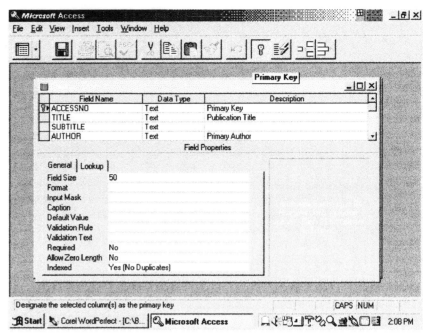

Figure 2.10 Primary Key

2.2 SAVING THE TABLE STRUCTURE

Now save your file structure.

Save

1. Click on the **Save** button in the tool bar or go to **File** on the menu bar and select **Save**. .

2. Access displays the box in which you name the table. Type "BOOKS".

3. Press **<Enter>** or click on OK.

The **Save** box in this case is different from other **Save file** dialog boxes you usually see in Windows programs. There is no way to specify a disk drive or other information besides the name. In Access, this table is considered part of a database (called **LIBRARY.MDB** in our case), and all the tables, queries and reports are considered part of that database. Disk drive and directory information are only entered when you save the database as a whole.

2.3 · CLOSING THE TABLE

The Access file structure has now been saved. You may start entering records, close the file, or exit Access. If you decide to close the file, do the following:

1. Click on **File** on the menu bar.

2. Click on **Close** (see Figure 2.11).

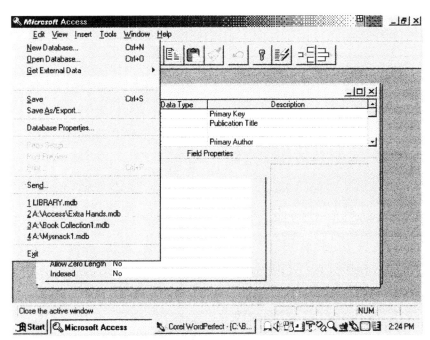

Figure 2.11 Closing the Table

2.4 EXITING ACCESS

If you want to end your Access session, do the following:

1. Click on **File** on the menu bar.

2. Click on **Exit** (see Figure 2.12).

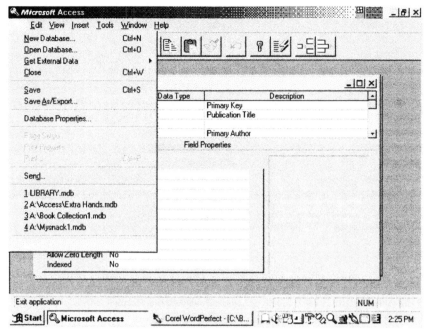

Figure 2.12 Exiting Access

2.5 OPENING ACCESS FILES

If you exited Access in the previous instructions, you now need to reopen Microsoft Access so you can start entering records. You should see the same blank Access screen as when you started (see Figure 2.1).

Open

1. Click on the **Open File** button in the speed bar.

Notice that the message "**Open an existing database**" appears in the status bar at the bottom of your screen.

2. Find **LIBRARY.MDB** in the file list and either double-click on the file name or click on the file name and then on OK (see Figure 2.13).

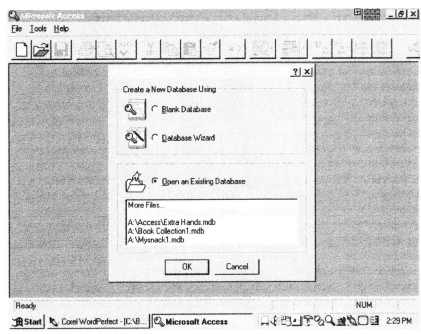

Figure 2.13 Open Existing Database

3.   Select BOOKS from the Tables list (see Figure 2.14).

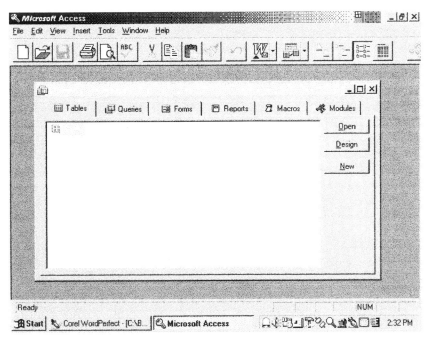

Figure 2.14 Selecting Table to Open

2.6 MODIFYING THE TABLE STRUCTURE

Now suppose that you start entering your books (records) into the **BOOKS** table and you quickly encounter one that has two authors, an illustrator, and an editor, each of whom merit separate entries in your catalog. Modifying the table structure is quite easy. Since you are looking at the screen used for data entry, you must first get back to the screen where we first designed the structure.

1.   Click on **Design** in the LIBRARY database list. Now you will see the screen displaying the database structure that you saw before when you designed the table (see Figure 2.15).

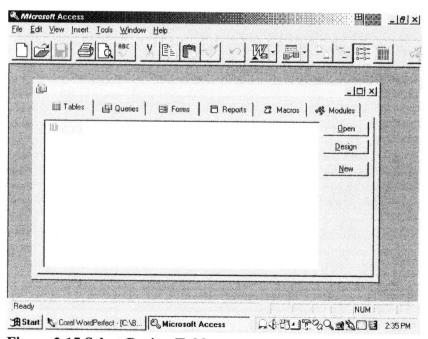

Figure 2.15 Select Design Table

We want a field for a second person whose name we want associated with the book in the catalog. Since we want this field to appear in a logical place in the structure, we will insert it there (see Figure 2.16).

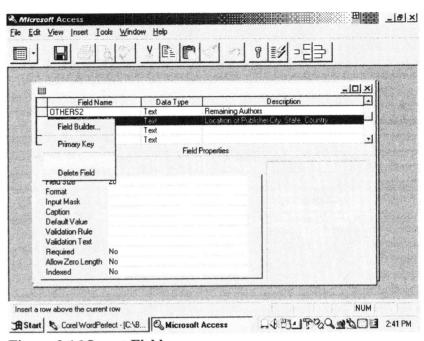

Figure 2.16 Insert Field

2.　　Click on the field name **Place_Published**.

3.　　Highlight and click on **Insert Field** menu item.

4.　　Enter the following field information into the table at this point:

Name: OTHERS2
Data Type: Text
Field length: 50

Save

5.　　**Save** the modified structure by clicking on the Save button on the speed bar.

6.　　**Close** the **Design** screen by clicking the **x** box in the upper right hand corner of the **Table Books** design screen.

2.7 Using the Table Wizard

Next we will use the Table Wizard feature of Access to design a table for library users.

1.   On the menu bar, click on **File** then **New Database** (see Figure 2.17).

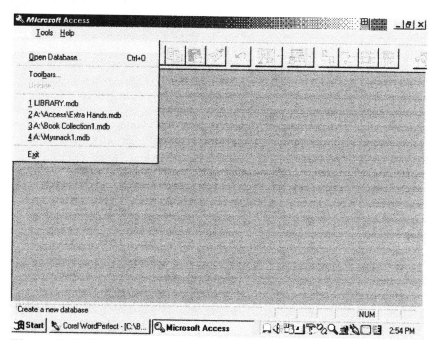

Figure 2.17 New Database

2.   Click on **Database Wizard** then **Table Wizard** (see Figures 2.18, 2.19).

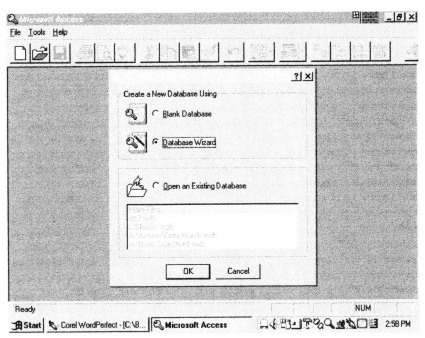

Figure 2.18 Database Wizard

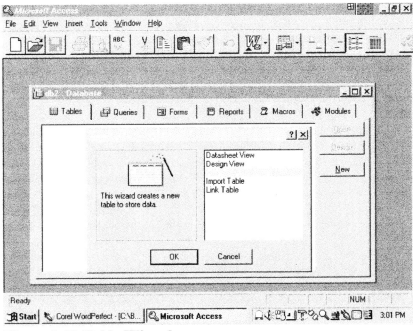

Figure 2.19 Table Wizard

The Wizard displays a list of possible database tables. There are tables for business and for personal purposes. From the business list, choose **Customers**. Each table in the list has a different list of possible fields.

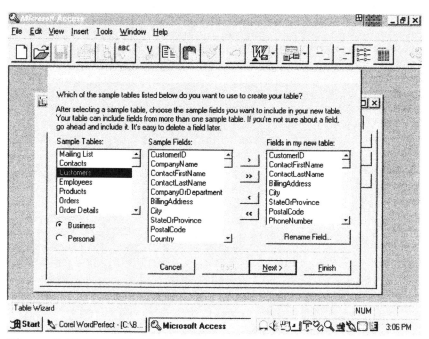

Figure 2.20 Data Field Selection

From the Customer list, choose these fields: (see Figure 2.20)

> **CustomerID**
> **ContactFirstName**
> **ContactLastName**
> **BillingAddress**
> **City**

StateOrProvince

PostalCode

PhoneNumber

Notes

3.　　Now click on **Next**. In this screen, name the table **LIBRARYUSERS**, and click on **No, I'll set the primary key** (see Figure 2.21).

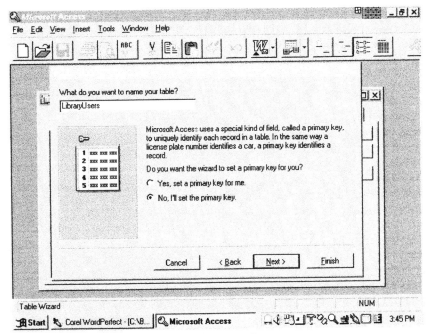

Figure 2.21 Table Wizard Primary Key

4. Click **Next** and Access displays a screen where you set the primary key. The first field on the list, **CUSTOMERID**, is the number that is unique to each library user, so we will use it as the primary key. Since the library already has a list of users with numbers already assigned, click the choice that says "**Numbers I enter when I add new records**" (see Figure 2.22).

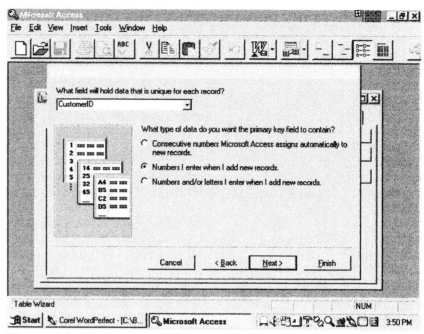

Figure 2.22 Primary Key Label

Click **Next**.

5.   In this screen, you opt either to modify the design
      or start entering records. Click "**Enter data
      directly into the table**"(see Figure 2.23).

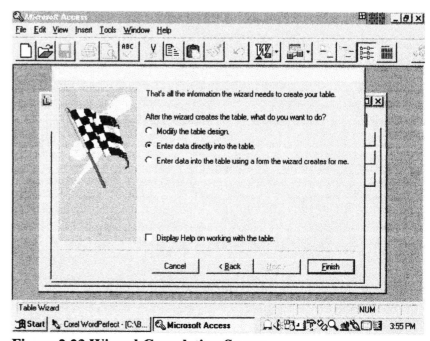

Figure 2.23 Wizard Completion Screen

Wizard

Wizard is the name of the Microsoft suite of products that comprise an online tutorial. These tutorials will lead you step by step through most any process, such as building a table, creating a report, or the like, that you may need to do in Access. We will not review Wizards in depth in this book because they are self explanatory when activated. You are encouraged to try using the Wizards for various aspects of database construction, as they can clarify questions for you and give you additional information on the process you are using.

CHAPTER 3 RECORDS

OBJECTIVES

3.1 ENTERING RECORDS

Open Microsoft Access. Select and open the BOOKS table
from the LIBRARY.MDB database (see Figure 3.1). You
should see an empty records screen. This is called the
Datasheet view (see Figure 3.2).

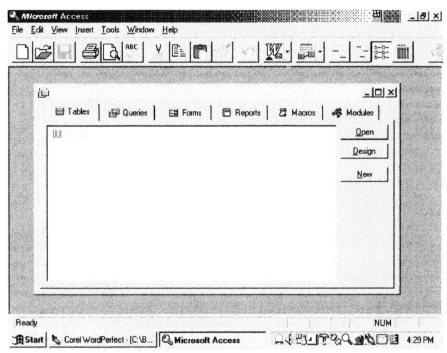

Figure 3.1 Table Selection Screen

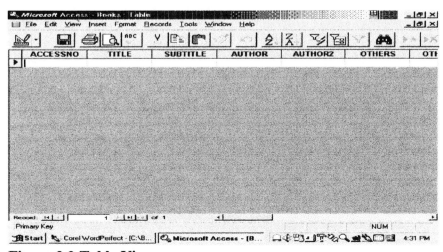

Figure 3.2 Table View

Open

1. Click on the **Open** button on the Library Database window.

2. Start entering data into the blank space specific to each field name. If you have designed well, you should be able to enter information easily.

3. When you finish entering data in a field, press <Enter> to move to the next blank field.

4. Access always places a blank record at the end of the record list. This record is designated by an asterisk in the column before the first field. The selected record is shown by an arrow head and a field with unsaved data is marked by a pencil (see Figure 3.3).

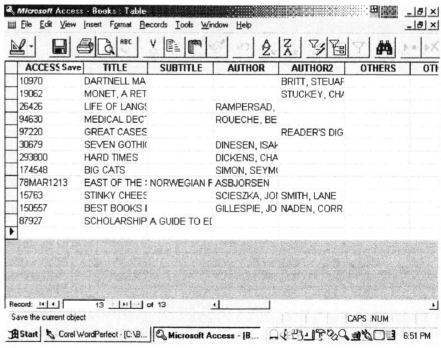

Figure 3.3 Table View With Data

5.   The **Notes** field, a field using the Memo data type, is handled exactly the same as other fields. Enter the data in the field. In many of the fields, you won't be able to see the whole entry, but it is there.

6.   Enter the information for the following books in the Books table.

LIST OF BOOKS:

ACCESSION:	19062
TITLE:	MONET, A RETROSPECTIVE
AUTHOR2:	STUCKEY, CHARLES F.
PLACE PUB:	NEW YORK, NY
PUBLISHER:	HUGH LAUTER LEVIN ASSOC. INC.
YR PUB:	1985
CALL NO:	O 7559.4 MON (oversized)
ISBN:	088363385X
SUBJ:	1. MONET, CLAUDE-1840-1926
	2. PAINTERS-FRANCE-BIOGRAPHY
NOTES:	PHYS. DESC.: 387P. ILL (SOME COLORED); 34 CM.

ACCESSION:	26426
TITLE:	LIFE OF LANGSTON HUGHES VOL 1
AUTHOR:	RAMPERSAD, ARNOLD
PLACE PUB:	NEW YORK, NY
PUBLISHER:	OXFORD UNIV. PRESS
YR PUB	1986
CALL NO:	818.52 RAM VOL 1
SUBJ:	1. HUGHES, LANGSTON-1902-1967-BIOGRAPHY
	2. POETS, AMERICAN-20TH CENTURY-BIOGRAPHY
NOTES:	PHYS DESC: V. 1 OF 2: ILL, PORTS. ; 24 CM
	CONTENTS: VOL 1: 1902-1941, I, TOO, SING AMERICA

ACCESSION:	10970

TITLE:	DARTNELL MARKETING MANAGER'S HANDBOOK
AUTHOR2:	BRITT, STEUART H. 1902-
PLACE PUB:	CHICAGO, ILL
PUBLISHER:	DARTNELL CORP.
YR PUB	1983
CALL NO:	658.8 DAR
ISBN:	0850131359
SUBJ:	1. MARKETING-MANAGEMENT
	2. MARKETING-HANDBOOKS, MANUALS, ETC.
NOTES:	PHYS DESC: 1293 P.: ILL; 23 CM.
	SERIES: DARTNELL HANDBOOKS
	TITLE VAR: MARKETING MANAGER'S HANDBOOK

ACCESSION:	94630
TITLE:	MEDICAL DETECTIVES
AUTHOR:	ROUECHE, BERTON, 1911-
PLACE PUB:	NEW YORK, NY
PUBLISHER:	NY TIMES BOOKS
YR PUB	1980
CALL NO:	610.926 ROU
ISBN:	0812909208
SUBJ:	1. EPIDEMIOLOGY-CASE STUDIES
	2. MEDICINE-CASE STUDIES
NOTES:	PHYS DESC: 372 P.; 24 CM.

ACCESSION:	97220
TITLE:	GREAT CASES OF SCOTLAND YARD
AUTHOR2	READERS DIGEST ASSN
PLACE PUB:	PLEASANTVILLE, NY
PUBLISHER:	READER'S DIGEST ASSN.
YR PUB:	1978
CALL NO:	345.421 GRE
ISBN:	0895770539
SUBJ:	1. GT BRITAIN-METROPOLITAN POLICE-CID
	2. CRIME AND CRIMINALS-GT BRITAIN--CASE STUDIES
	3. CRIMINAL INVESTIGATION-GT BRITAIN-CASE STUDIES
NOTES:	PHYS DESC: 690 P. (5) LEAVES OF

PLATES: ILL ; 24 CM
1ST EDITION

ACCESSION:	30679
TITLE:	SEVEN GOTHIC TALES
AUTHOR	DINESEN, ISAK
PLACE PUB:	NEW YORK, NY
PUBLISHER:	MODERN LIBRARY
YR PUB:	1961
CALL NO:	F DIN
NOTES:	COPYRIGHT: 1934
	PHYS DESC: 420 P. ILL. ; 20 CM
	CONTENTS: THE DELUGE AT NORDERNEY- THE OLD CHEVALIER- THE MONKEY- THE ROADS ROUND PISA- THE SUPPER AT ELSINORE- THE DREAMERS-- THE POETS.

ACCESSION:	293800
TITLE:	HARD TIMES
AUTHOR:	DICKENS, CHARLES
PLACE PUB	LONDON, GB
PUBLISHER:	COLLINS
YR PUB	1959
CALL NO	F DIC
NOTES:	PHYS DESC: 288 P. PORT.
	SERIES: COLLINS CLASSICS

ACCESSION:	174548
TITLE:	BIG CATS
AUTHOR:	SIMON, SEYMOUR
PLACE PUB:	NEW YORK, NY
PUBLISHER:	HARPERCOLLINS
YR PUB	1991
CALL NO:	J 599.744 SIM
ISBN:	0060216476
SUBJ:	1. FELIDAE-JUVENILE LITERATURE
	2. CATS
	3. BLUEBONNET BOOK-1992-1993
NOTES:	PHYS DESC: 40 P. COL. ILL. ; 24X29 CM

ACCESSION: 78MAR1213
TITLE: EAST O' THE SUN AND WEST O' THE
                  MOON
SUBTITLE: NORWEGIAN FOLK TALES
AUTHOR: ASBJORNSEN
PLACE PUB: GARDEN CITY, NY
PUBLISHER: NELSON DOUBLEDAY
YR PUB: 1957
NOTES: PHYS DESC: 288 P. : 1LL. ; 22 CM.
                  EDITION: JUNIOR DELUXE EDITION

ACCESSION: 15763
TITLE: STINKY CHEESE MAN AND OTHER
                  FAIRLY STUPID TALES
AUTHOR: SCIESZKA, JON
AUTHOR2:   SMITH, LANE
PLACE PUB: NEW YORK, NY
PUBLISHER: VIKING
YR PUB   1992
CALL NO   J F SCI
ISBN: 067084487X
SUBJ: 1 FAIRY TALES-UNITED STATES
                  2. CHILDREN'S STORIES, AMERICAN
                  3. BLUEBONNET BOOK-1994-95
NOTES: PHYS DESC: 1 V. (UNPAGED); COL.
                  ILL.; 28 CM.

ACCESSION: 150557
TITLE: BEST BOOKS FOR CHILDREN,
                  PRESCHOOL THROUGH GR. 6
AUTHOR: GILLESPIE, JOHN THOMAS
AUTHOR2:   NADEN, CORRINE J.
PLACE PUB: NEW YORK, NY
PUBLISHER: R. R. BOWKER
YR PUB: 1990
CALL NO: J REF 011.62 GIL
ISBN: 0835226689
SUBJ: 1. BIBLIOGRAPHY-BEST BOOKS-
                  CHILDREN'S
                  2. CHILDREN'S LITERATURE-
                  BIBLIOGRAPHY
                  3. LIBRARIES, CHILDREN'S-BOOK
                  LIST

NOTES:	PHYS DESC: 1002 P.
	EDITION: 4TH EDITION

ACCESSION:	87927
TITLE:	SCHOLARSHIPS, FELLOWSHIPS, AND LOANS:
SUBTITLE:	A GUIDE TO EDUCATION-RELATED FINANCIAL AID PROGRAMS
PLACE PUB:	DETROIT, MI
PUBLISHER:	GALE RESEARCH
YR PUB:	1992
CALL NO:	REF 378.3
SUBJ:	1. SCHOLARSHIPS-UNITED STATES -DIRECTORIES
	2. STUDENT LOAN FUNDS-UNITED STATES-DIRECTORIES
	3. COLLEGE COSTS-UNITED STATES
NOTES:	EDITION: 9TH EDITION, FIRST GALE EDITION

Figure 3.4 shows the Datasheet view of the table with records entered. The fields not showing in the screen can be found by using the scroll bars at the bottom of the screen. The arrows on the left move the cursor among the records, one record at a time, or to the beginning or end of the records entered. The right portion of the scroll bar moves the cursor among the fields in the selected record.

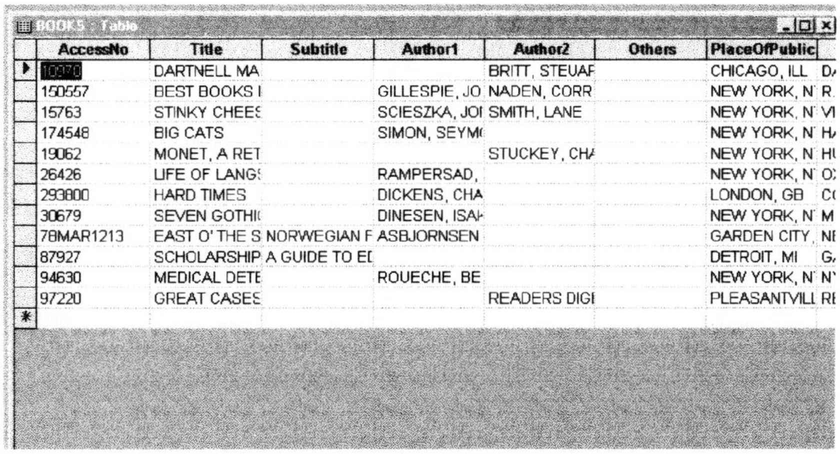

Figure 3.4 DataSheet View of Records Entered

3.2 DELETING RECORDS

Suppose that after entering these twelve books, you notice the book *East o' the Sun and West o' the Moon* has an accession number that does not follow the pattern of the accession numbers in your library and actually belongs to another library. Open the Books table in the Datasheet mode by clicking on the button that allows you to "**Display the document in Datasheet view**." (see Figure 3.5).

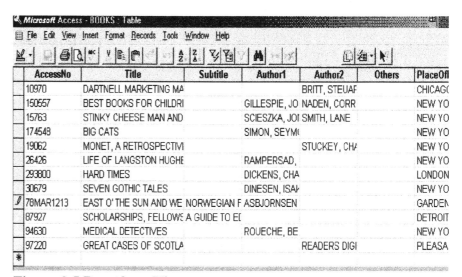

AccessNo	Title	Subtitle	Author1	Author2	Others	PlaceOf
10970	DARTNELL MARKETING MA			BRITT, STEUAF		CHICAG(
150557	BEST BOOKS FOR CHILDRI		GILLESPIE, JO	NADEN, CORR		NEW YO
15763	STINKY CHEESE MAN AND		SCIESZKA, JOI	SMITH, LANE		NEW YO
174548	BIG CATS		SIMON, SEYM(			NEW YO
19062	MONET, A RETROSPECTIVI			STUCKEY, CH/		NEW YO
26426	LIFE OF LANGSTON HUGHE		RAMPERSAD,			NEW YO
293800	HARD TIMES		DICKENS, CHA			LONDON
30679	SEVEN GOTHIC TALES		DINESEN, ISA|			NEW YO
78MAR1213	EAST O' THE SUN AND WE	NORWEGIAN F	ASBJORNSEN			GARDEN
87927	SCHOLARSHIPS, FELLOWS	A GUIDE TO EI				DETROIT
94630	MEDICAL DETECTIVES		ROUECHE, BE			NEW YO
97220	GREAT CASES OF SCOTL^				READERS DIGI	PLEASA

Figure 3.5 Datasheet View

You only have a few records entered at this point, so it will be easy to just browse through them until you find the one you want- *East o' the Sun and West o' the Moon*. Delete this record:

1. Click on this record.

2. Click on **Edit** in the menu list. Click on **Select Record** to highlight it (see Figure 3.6).

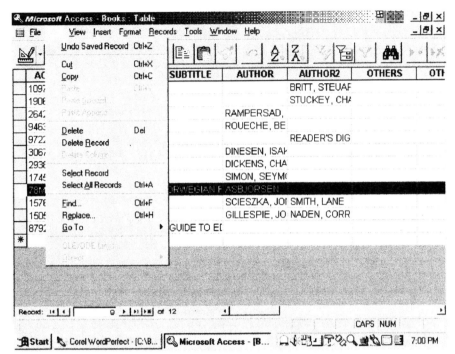

Figure 3.6 Delete Selected Records

3.   Press the <Delete> key on your keyboard or delete using the pull down menu.

Notice that the record and record number vanish immediately (see Figure 3.7). Access displays a message screen asking you to confirm that you want to delete this record or group of records.

4.   Click **OK**.

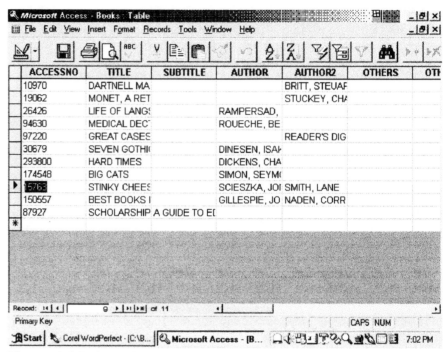

Figure 3.7 Deleted Record Datasheet View

3.3 FINDING RECORDS

Later in this manual, you will be working with ways to manipulate the checkout or circulation records in your library. Use the **Find** feature on the speed bar to locate book records and enter user numbers in the UserNo field, "Y" in the Checkout field, and dates in the DateChek field.

Find

1. Click on the **AccessNo** field in the first record to indicate that this is where you want Access to look for the indicated formation. Click on the **Find** button in the speed bar to open the **Find Records** dialog box (see Figure 3.8).

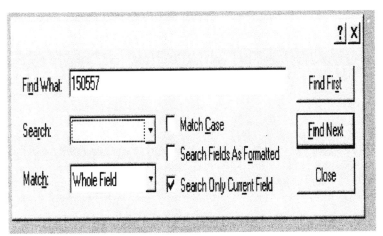

Figure 3.8 Find Records Dialog Box

2.   Type "150557" in the **Fi_n_d What** box.

3.   In **Match** select **Whole Field**.

4.   Click **Search Only Current Field** in the **Search In** box, and **Down** in the **Search Box.**

5.   Click on the **Find Fir_s_t** button. Access immediately locates the record requested, shows the dialog box with the correct choices, and highlights the matching record (see Figure 3.9).

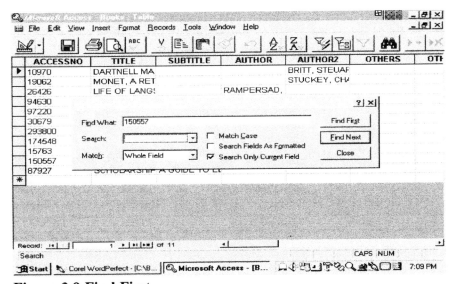

Figure 3.9 Find First

6.   Close the **Find Records** box.

7.   Scroll across and enter "Y" in the **Checkout** field, "35986" in the **UserNo** field, and "04/03/95" in the **DateChek** field.

Repeat steps 1 through 5 and add the following checkout information.

ACCESSNO	USERNO	DATECHEK
30679	74624	03/30/95
97220	46873	03/27/95
10907	87234	03/31/95
19062	74624	01/24/95

This covers entering records, deleting records, and finding records using Access. You are now prepared to do further manipulations of your data such as sorting records, filtering, selection criteria, and complicated sorts. These procedures can simplify library operations by providing the tools to manage and display the data in the records in a variety of ways. The next chapter will cover sorting your records, including filtering, selection criteria, and complicated sorts.

CHAPTER 4 SORTS

OBJECTIVES

4.1 SORTING RECORDS

4.2 FILTERING

4.3 SELECTION CRITERIA

4.4 COMPLICATED SORT

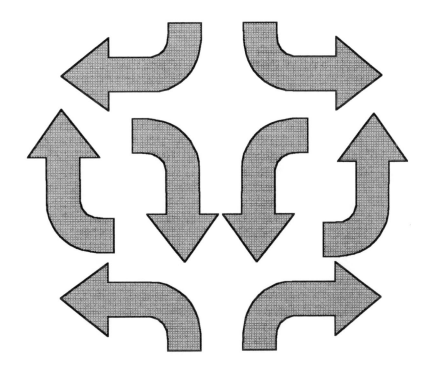

Sorting and filters are two different methods of putting records in order. Each method has its advantages and disadvantages. Sorting allows you only to sort all the data in a particular table. Filtering allows you to exclude information. Both methods allow only temporary changes. To make permanent changes, use Query (chapter 5) and Reports (chapter 6).

4.1   Sorting Records

Before we begin with the sort function, we will add records to the LIBRARYUSER table. Open the LIBRARYUSER table (see chapter 2, "Tables", for instructions).

Enter the following records in the **LIBRARYUSER** table.

CUSTOMER ID:	39876
LASTNAME:	BURTON
FIRSTNAME:	WILLIAM
ADDRESS:	692 REDBIRD AVE #2
CITY:	MANCHESTER
STATE:	KY
POSTAL CODE:	40477

CUSTOMER ID:	35986
LASTNAME:	BURTON
FIRSTNAME:	ELIZABETH
ADDRESS:	692 REDBIRD AVE #2
CITY:	MANCHESTER
STATE:	KY
POSTAL CODE:	40477

CUSTOMER ID:	74624
LASTNAME:	BURTON
FIRSTNAME:	BONNIE
ADDRESS:	692 REDBIRD AVE #2
CITY:	MANCHESTER
STATE:	KY
POSTAL CODE:	40477

CUSTOMER ID:	46873
LASTNAME:	THOMPSON
FIRSTNAME:	THELMA
ADDRESS:	2515 MAGNOLIA CT.
CITY:	COALMINE
STATE:	KY
POSTAL CODE:	40798

CUSTOMER ID:	56734
LASTNAME:	CROW
FIRSTNAME:	TRACE
ADDRESS:	249 MOONBEEM DR.
CITY:	COALMINE
STATE:	KY
POSTAL CODE:	40798

CUSTOMER ID:	87905
LASTNAME:	HELMINTH
FIRSTNAME:	HERMAN
ADDRESS:	5629 HUNSDALE ST.
CITY:	CORVIN
STATE:	KY
POSTAL CODE:	40879

CUSTOMER ID:	87234
LASTNAME:	WHITE
FIRSTNAME:	BLANCHE
ADDRESS:	984 BLANCO LN.
CITY:	CORVIN
STATE:	KY
POSTAL CODE:	40879

CUSTOMER ID:	56498
LASTNAME:	CROW
FIRSTNAME:	BOBBIE
ADDRESS:	456 MAINSTAY ST.
CITY:	DANVILLE
STATE:	KY
POSTAL CODE:	79823

OPEN

There are several reasons why a library would want a list of library users sorted according to where they live. For example, the library might be considering a new location for a branch and the management of the library might want to consider only those areas that have current library users. Or perhaps the library is planning special events to be held in different user areas.

To create a sorted table, follow the directions below:

1.   Open the LIBRARYUSER table (see Figure 4.1).

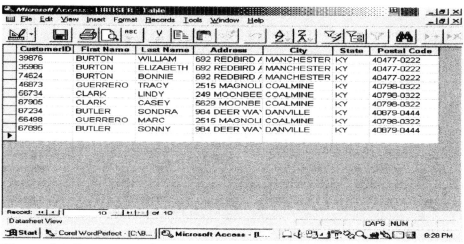
Figure 4.1 Open LIBUSER Table

2.   Click on the top of the **POSTAL CODE** field, so the cursor turns into a down arrow (see Figure 4.2).

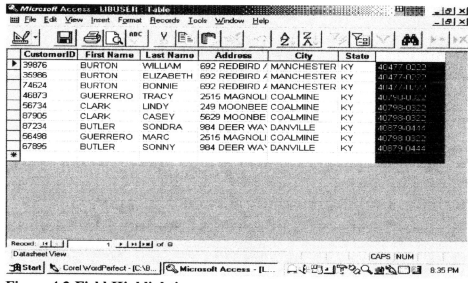
Figure 4.2 Field Highlighting

Sort
Ascending

3.   Click the Sort Ascending toolbar, which arranges the table in numerical order according to the zip code (see Figure 4.3).

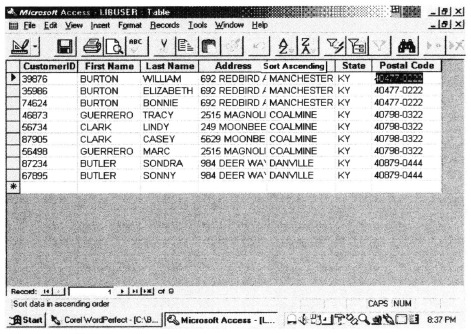

Figure 4.3 Sorting

The sort shows Postal Codes in numerical order. Notice that the Postal Codes with the same number are not sorted in any particular order such as alphabetically by first name.

4.   Click on the top of **LASTNAME** so the field is highlighted, then drag the mouse (holding the left mouse button down) over to **FIRSTNAME** until the field is highlighted (see Figure 4.4).

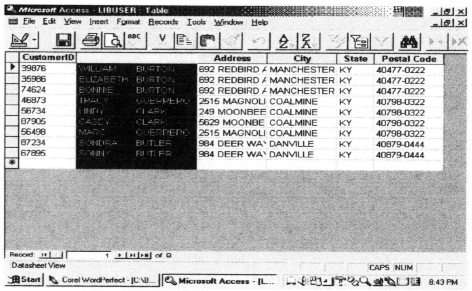

Figure 4.4 Sorting Multiple Fields

5.   Click **Records**, then **Sort**, then **Ascending** (see Figure 4.5).

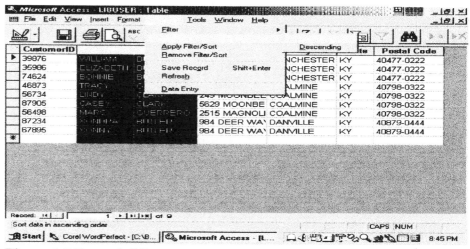

Figure 4.5 Records Menu

6.   Notice the table is now sorted by Postal Code, then by First Name and Last Name (see Figure 4.6).

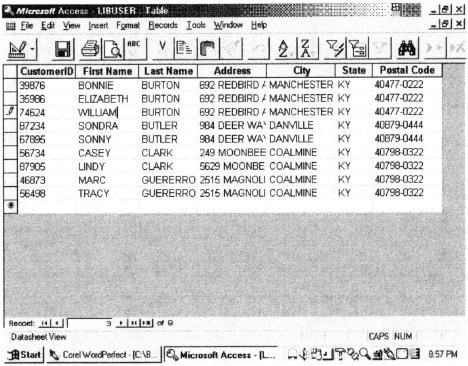

Figure 4.6 Results of Sort

4.2 FILTERING

Filter

Filtering allows you to sort the data and view only the desired records. For example, this function would be useful if the library wanted to see exactly how many users have checked out books. Keep in mind that filtering is only temporary and cannot be saved with the table. To create a table that could be saved and linked with other tables, see chapter 5, "Queries". To filter the records so only the users that have checked out books are shown, follow the steps below.

1.   Open the BOOKS table.

OPEN

2.   Click **Records** on the menu bar, then click **Advanced Filter/Sort** (see Figure 4.7).

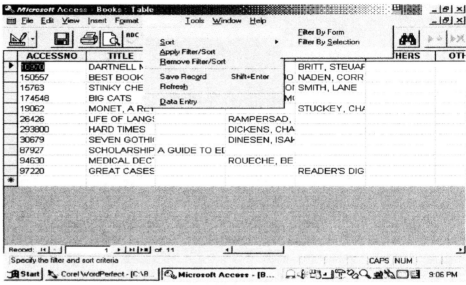

Figure 4.7 Filter Sort

3.   The top portion of the filter screen includes a list of all the fields in the BOOKS table. Scroll down and double click on the **CHECKOUT** field (see Figure 4.8).

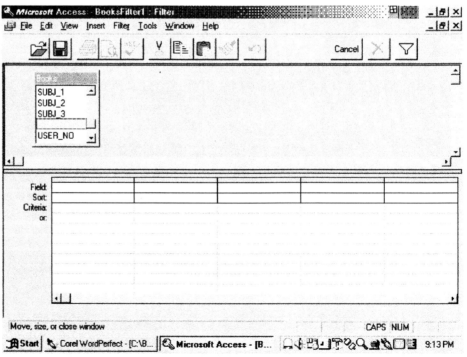

Figure 4.8 Select Sort Field

4.	Using the mouse, click in the **S**ort field directly below Filter, in the bottom portion of the filter screen (see Figure 4.9).

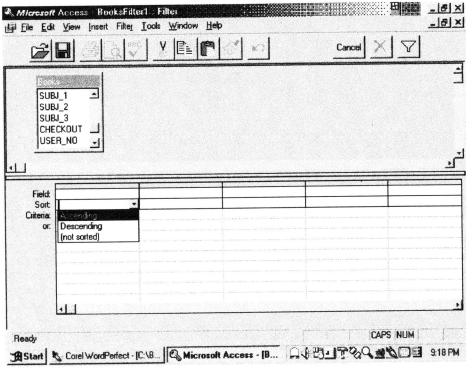

Figure 4.9 Sort Criteria

5.	Click the down arrow that appears on the right , then select **Ascending** (see Figure 4.10).

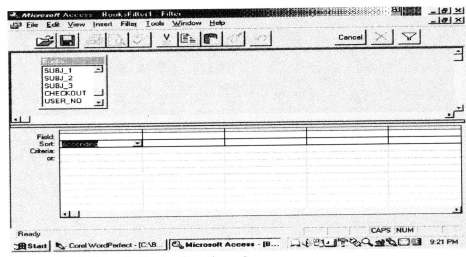

Figure 4.10 Sort Criteria Continued

6. Click the **Criteria** box that is directly beneath the sort field. Type in the word **"Yes"**. This will allow the sort to include only the books that have been checked out to appear (see Figure 4.11).

7. Click the **Apply Filter** sort button (see Figure 4.11).

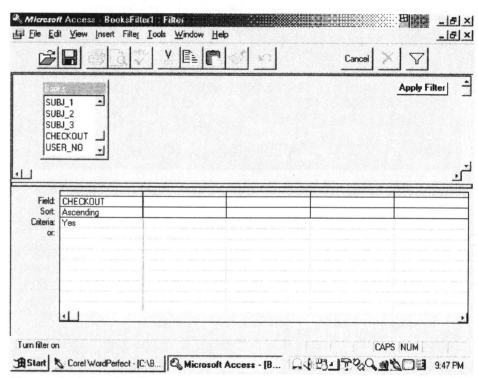

Figure 4.11 Apply Filter

8. When you have finished using the filter to restore the table to its original format, click **Records** from the top menu bar, then click **Remove Filter Sort** (see Figure 4.12).

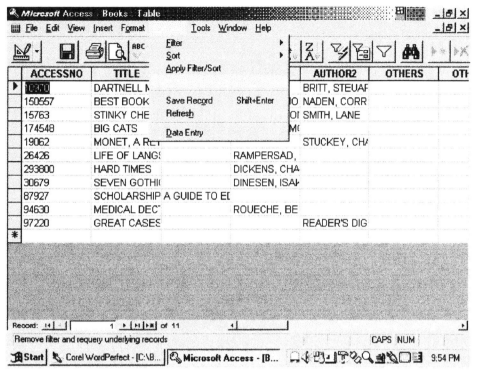

Figure 4.12 Filter/Sort

4.3   SELECTION CRITERIA

Understanding the filter criteria will help the user to create a filter containing only the required information. For instance, the previous example used criteria to select only those individuals who had checked out books.

Using other criteria, you can sort data by a value or a range of values. Using the chart below will assist in determining how to enter the criteria.

INPUTS	DESCRIPTION
=	Equal to
<>	Not equal to
>	Greater than
<	Less than

>=	Greater than or equal to
<=	Less than or equal to
Between...And	Between two specified values
Is Null	Doesn't contain data
Like	Matches a pattern containing wildcard characters

Using the table as a guide for the criteria of the filter, you can obtain exactly the information you require. For example, if you want only the people who checked out books on March 25, 1996, in the criteria field, you would type = 3/25/1996.

4.4 Complicated Sort

This sort will demonstrate how to further utilize sorting criteria in sorting: display only the users in Manchester, KY with User numbers greater than 40000.

1. Open the **LIBUSER** table (see Figure 4.13).

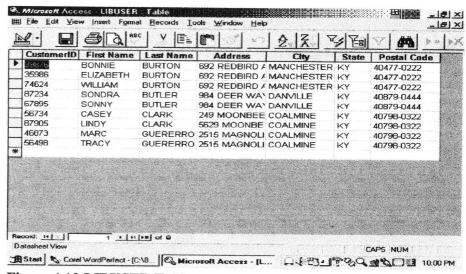

Figure 4.13 LIBUSER Table

2. Click **Records**, then **Advanced Filter/Sort** (see Figure 4.14).

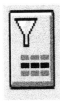

Filter

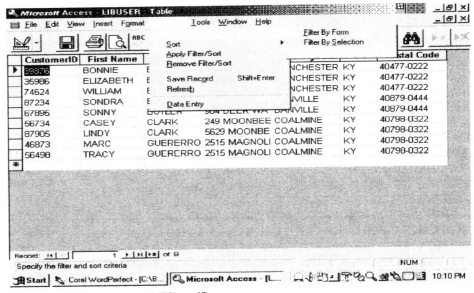

Figure 4.14 Advanced Filter/Sort

3. Double click on **CustomerID, FirstName, LastName**, and **City.**

4. To create the sort with the criteria of only those individuals in Manchester, click **Criteria** under City, then type in Manchester.

5. In order to include only those people in Manchester with CustomerID numbers greater than 40000, click on **Criteria** under CustomerID and type ">40000" (see Figure 4.15).

6. Click on the **Sort** column under **FirstName** and enter **Ascending**, then do the same for **LastName** (see Figure 4.15).

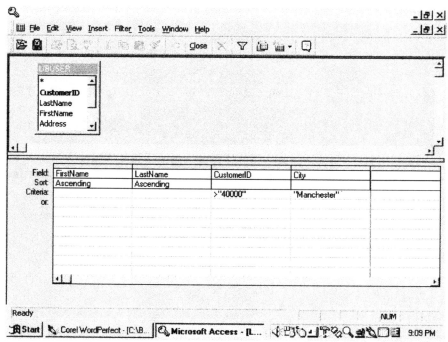

Figure 4.15 Select Sort Criteria

7. Click on **Apply Filter** (see Figure 4.16).

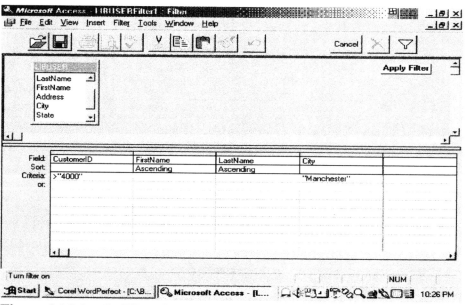

Figure 4.16 Apply Filter Sort

This sort shows only those individuals in Manchester whose CustomerID numbers are greater than 40000. There was only one customer meeting these criteria (see Figure 4.17).

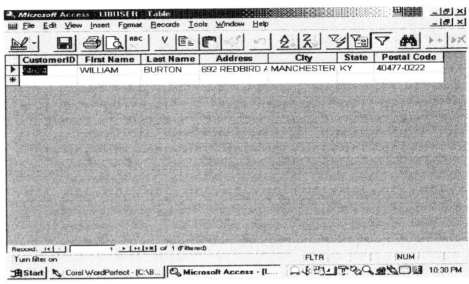

Figure 4.17 Results Screen

Filtering is used when the selection is needed temporarily. When more permanent data manipulations are needed, Queries (discussed in chapter 5) offers yet another way to extract information from your database.

Sorting can accomplish many different things. Every field in the database can be sorted for ease of use. One of the primary purposes of database management systems is to retrieve information in ways that are the most useful to the users of the system. In the next chapter we will discuss how to set up a query to retrieve information.

CHAPTER 5 QUERIES

OBJECTIVES

In chapter 4, use of the **Find** command to access a single record was demonstrated. Query allows you to display a certain grouping of records and certain fields in those records. The query function compares each record to the filter requirements, keeping or discarding records for the new query file. When a query has been designed for a specific purpose, such as an author search, you can save it and use it again for other author searches. You can also use query to create a report. A query is a one time gathering of information, whereas a report is data that will be used on a regular basis.

In past chapters, you have worked with tables. Queries look at information in the database. As with a table, you can choose display formats (Browse, Form, or Columnar). Creating a query using more than one file will be explained in chapter 6.

5.1   CREATE A QUERY

Create a new query the same way you would create any other item, for example a table.

1.   **Open** Access to the **LIBRARY.MDB** database window (See Figure 5.1).

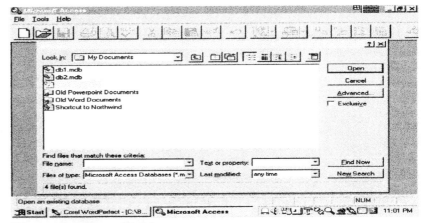

Figure 5.1 Open Table

2.   Click **Queries.** The selection area will be blank because this is the first query being created (see Figure 5.2).

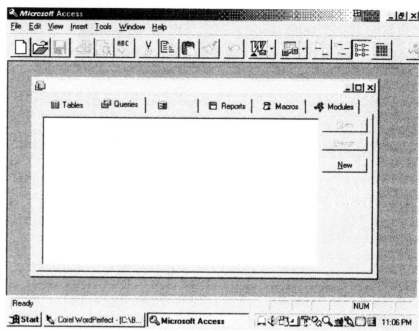

Figure 5.2 Select Query

3.   Click **New** (see Figure 5.2).

4.   Choose **Design View** (see Figure 5.3). All the tables under the library database will appear in a **Show Table** window.

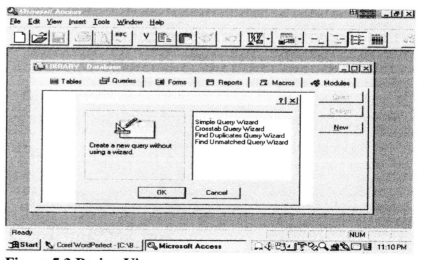

Figure 5.3 Design View

5. Double click on **Library Users** (see Figure 5.4).

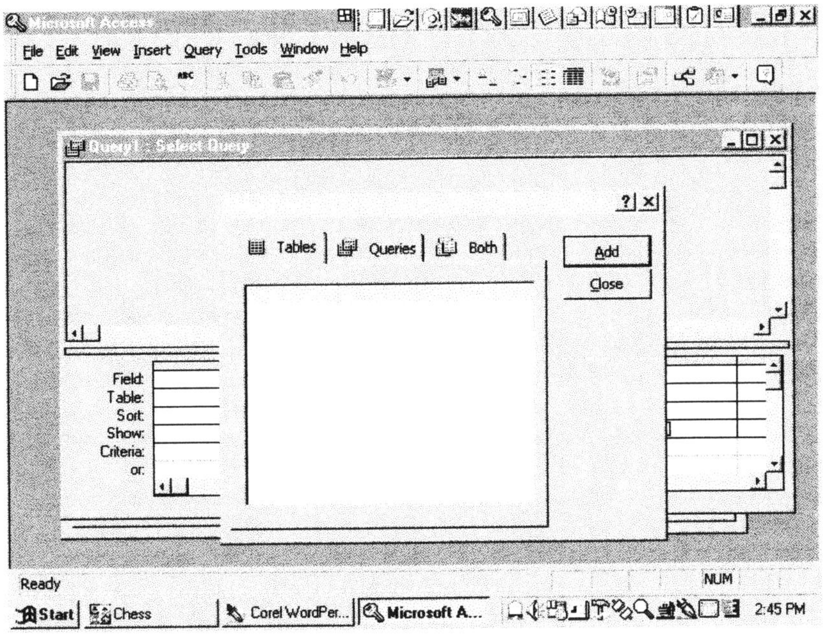

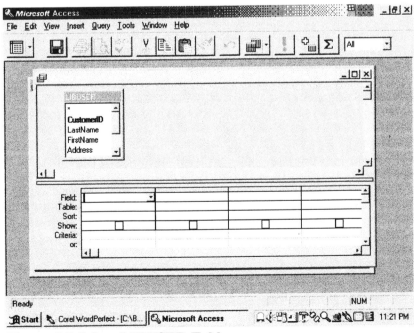

Figure 5.4 LIBUSER Table Query

6. **C**lose the **Show Table Window** (see Figure 5.5).

Figure 5.5 Select LIBUSER Table

7. Double click the **FirstName** field, then click on the box below the field name and sort **Ascending**. Follow the figures below to continue creating fields (see Figures 5.6, 5.7).

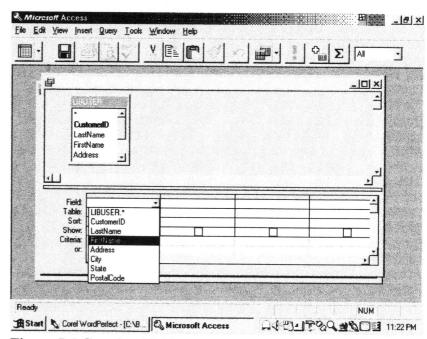

Figure 5.6 Creating Fields

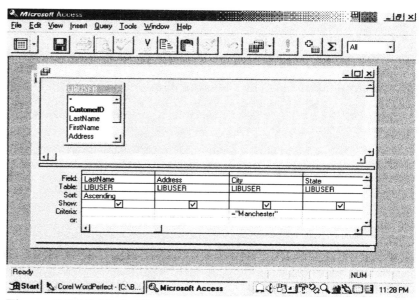

Figure 5.7 Multiple Fields

Run

8.   Select the **Run** button from the toolbar (see Figures 5.8, 5.9).

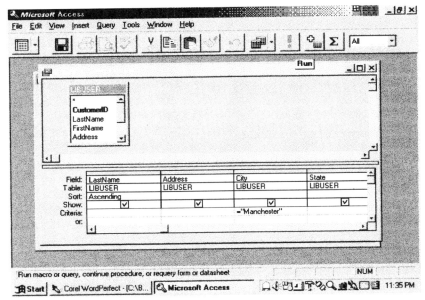

Figure 5.8 Run Query

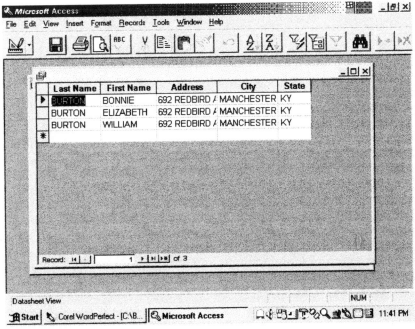

Figure 5.9 Query Results

9.   Click **File** on the menu bar, then click **Save As**, and finally name the query "**Manchester**."

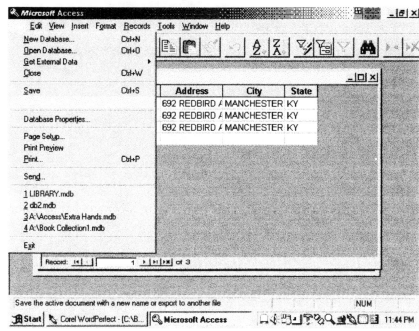

Figure 5.10 Save As

10.   Click on **OK**.

These instructions created a query that included only those library users from Manchester.

5.2   A Simple Query

1.   Open Microsoft Access, and open the **Library** database.

2.   Click **Queries**, **NEW**, then **Design View** (not Query Wizard) (see Figures 5.11, 5.12).

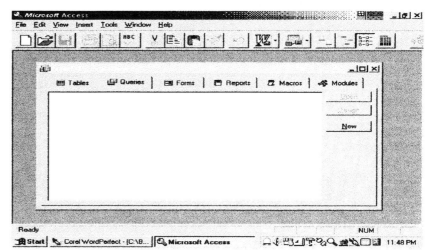

Figure 5.11 Simple Query

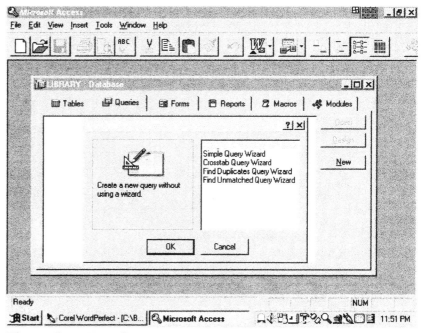

Figure 5.12 New Query

3.   Click on the Books table, then **close** the **Show Table** box (see figure 5.13).

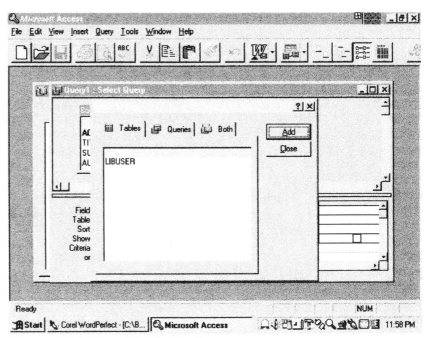

Figure 5.13 Open Table for Query

4.   As this query is only to show books that have been checked out, double click CHECKOUT, and under Criteria type "Yes" . Now double click: **Title, Author, CallNo, CustomerID and Datecheck** (see Figure 5.14).

5.   Under Title, click on **Sort** and sort in **Ascending order** (see Figure 5.14).

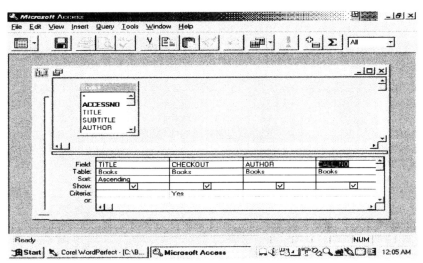

Figure 5.14 Sort Query

Run

6. Click the **Run** button to display the results (see Figure 5.15).

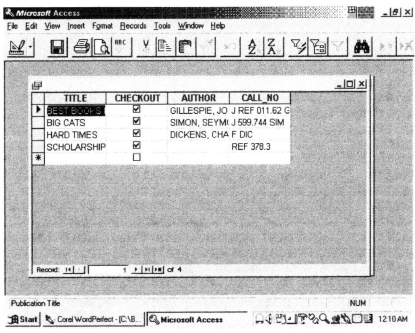

Figure 5.15 Run Query

7. Click the **Design** button, and add an additional condition to the query.

8.   Click on **Criteria** under **DateDue**, type
      ="1/24/95". This will include only those books
      that are due on that particular date.

9.   Click **File**.

10.   Click on **Save Query As.**

11.   Type **"OverDue"** as the file name, then click **OK.**

5.3 Complex Query

We usually think of logical or mathematical concepts as
applying to numbers. However, when used as a
comparison (or relational) operator, they can affect
character fields also. **Ascending** order is A through Z,
so B is greater than A. The following is an example of B
being greater then A.

1.   Create a new query: Click **Queries** and **New.**

2.   Click on the **BOOKS** table and close the **Show
      Table** window.

3.   Click **Title**, and type **"<B"** in the criteria field
      (see Figure 5.16).

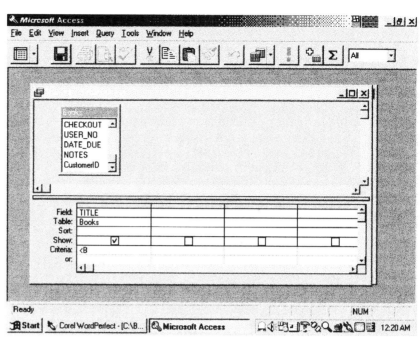

Figure 5.16 Entering Criteria

Run

4.   Click the **Run** button to display the query. Since there are no books with the title beginning with A, the query was empty (see Figure 5.17).

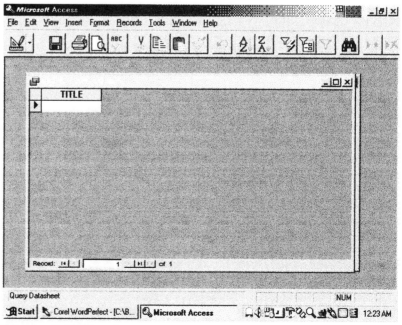

Figure 5.17 Results

For example, if a user is looking for a book and all he remembers is that it's about Monet's paintings and it's a big book. He's sure the title contains the word "Monet". If the criteria contained any type of punctuation it would then be necessary to place it in quotes. For example Monet does not have to have quotation marks, but if you were looking for Monet, Michael you would, because of the comma between Monet and Michael.

Design

5.   Click the **Design** button.

6.   Change the <B in the **Criteria** field to ">= Monet". Since the word Monet contains no punctuation, it is not necessary to place quotation marks around the word (see Figure 5.18).

7.   To complete the query, click the following field names: Title, Author, Call<u>N</u>o, and ISBN.

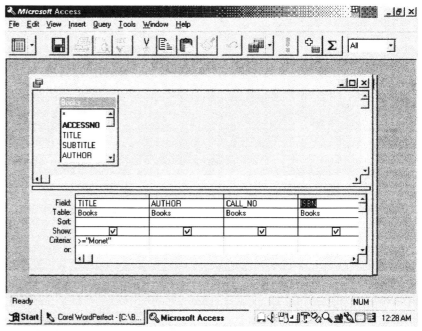

Figure 5.18 Selecting Fields

8. Click **Run** to execute the query (see Figure 5.19).

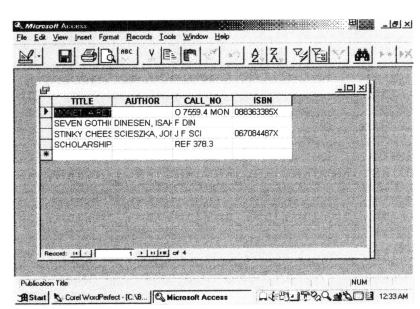

Figure 5.19 Query Results

5.4 RENAME A QUERY

Let's say that after a file has been saved, you decide that the name of the query or file isn't what you need or wanted. Changing a file name is as easy as saving the file. Let's change the file for overdue books and create a query for books in the library.

1. Open the query OVERDUE if you saved it earlier. If not, create another query for overdue books and save it with a new name.

Design

2. Click the **Design** button.

3. As we are changing the Overdue file to books in the library, the needs of the query have changed. The fields **CustomerID** and **Date_Due** are no longer needed. To delete these fields, just highlight them by clicking the mouse button; when

the mouse button changes to the down arrow, press the <Delete> key on the keyboard.

4.   Add the **ISBN** field by clicking in the field next to **CallNo** (it should be empty). Use the pull down menu by clicking the down arrow in this field. Click **ISBN**. Now there is a new field in our query.

5.   To change from books checked out of the library to books in the library, click in the criteria field of Checkout and type "**NO**".

6.   **Run** the query.

7.   Click **File, Save Query As,** and name the field type "In Library" (see Figure 5.20).

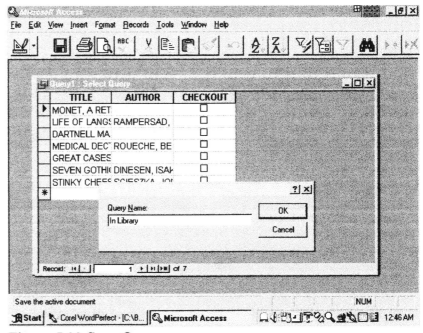

Figure 5.20 Save Query

8.   Close query window by clicking **Close**.

9.   Let's change the name of **In Library** to **BOOKS In**. Click **File**, **Rename,** and type **"BOOKS IN"**. Then click **OK**.

As queries are one type of information retrieval, the need for reports exist for recurring information. Queries are used primarily for onetime information and ad hoc kinds of reports; reports are primarily for recurring information requirements. Reports are discussed next in chapter 6.

CHAPTER 6

RELATIONAL DATABASES

OBJECTIVES

      6.1   RELATIONS

      6.2   RELATED TABLES

You now know how to: search the catalog you created in Access for books satisfying certain criteria, construct a shelf list, find a list of checked out books, determine the due date of checked out books, and identify the user numbers of the users who have them. The next step is to combine these functions to create a list of books with the names and addresses of those who have checked them out. You will accomplish this by relating databases known as Relational Databases. Relational Databases is a method of combining information in different tables and linking the tables using a common field. We will create a list of users who have overdue books using this method.

Assume we have a list of the books in the library, and we also have a list of users. If we considered only the information we're gathering and not how we plan to use it, we would probably duplicate information that we enter into the database. Without planning, for example, we might have created the tables so that every time a book was checked out the user's name would have to be typed in, which is a waste of valuable resources, disk space, and staff time. Data Normalization is the process of organizing your data structure to preclude entering more information than necessary or to avoid excessive duplication. To link BOOKS with LIBUSER tables so we can find out who has checked out what and what is checked out to whom, we put the CustomerID field in both tables.

Note
When deciding which field should be used in linking, you must choose carefully. Never use a field that changes or might be confused with another field. For example, **LASTNAME** might be a logical choice, but names can change, and more than one person can have the same last name. Social Security numbers are specific

to each person, but young people don't always have Social Security numbers. Each volume in the library also has an assigned number, the accession number, whose sole purpose is to identify one specific copy of a title; therefore the unique number to use for linking tables could be the accession.

6.1 RELATIONS

There are three different kinds of relations in relational database design.

- One-to-one relation: unique link between two items, not shared by any other relation. The relationship between each user and the user number, or between each book and its accession number, is unique. An example would be one customer may only check out one book. One-to-one, one book per customer.

- One-to-many: link to one item that may be shared by many items in the same way. The relation of the user to the books is one-to-many items in the same way. The relation of the user to the books is one-to-many because one user may check out many books. You usually don't have one person checking out multiple copies of the same title. This time one customer may check out many books - one-to-many relationship.

- Many-to-many: most tables have a many-to-many link. Each user may check out many books, and tracking library circulation over time, each book may have been checked out by many users.

6.2 RELATED TABLES

For the relation between the two tables to work correctly, each user must have a **unique** identifier, and each book checked out must have the user's identifier entered in its record. Otherwise, the tables won't link correctly.

The first step is to create a query that includes the two tables we wish to relate. Microsoft Access will look up each record in the table and pick out those records that meet the criteria presented in the query.

1.   Click on **Queries**, then **New** (see Figure 6.1).

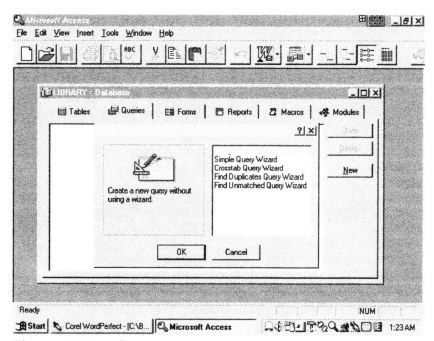

Figure 6.1 New Query

Design

2.   Select and click on **Design View.**

3.   Select LIBUSER, then BOOKS (see Figure 6.2).

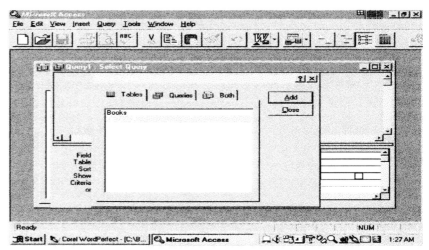

Figure 6.2 Select Tables

4.   Close the **Show Table** window.

5.   In BOOKS, click the down arrow until
        CustomerID appears.

6.   In LIBRARY USERS, click on **CustomerID** and
        hold down the left mouse button and drag it over
        CustomerID in the **BOOKS** table, then let go.
        There should be a line connecting the two fields
        (see Figure 6.3).

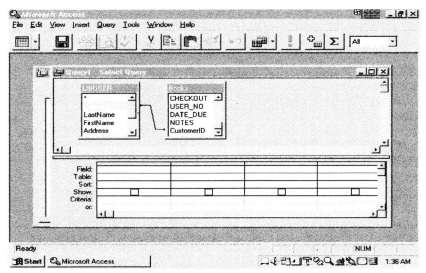

Figure 6.3 Link Tables

7. Select the following fields in the **LIBUSERS** table: **FirstName, LastName, Address, City, State, and Postal Code**.

8. Select the following fields in the BOOKS table: **AccessNo, Title, CallNo, CheckOut** (see Figure 6.4).

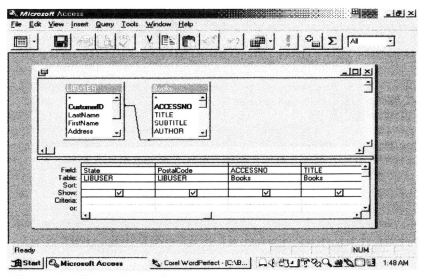

Figure 6.4 Select Criteria

Run

9.   Click the **Run** button (see Figure 6.5).

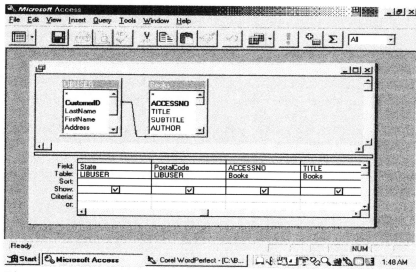

Figure 6.5 Run Query

10.   Click on **Design**.

11.   Select **Date_Due** criteria and enter 4/03/96.

Run

12.   Run query (see Figure 6.6).

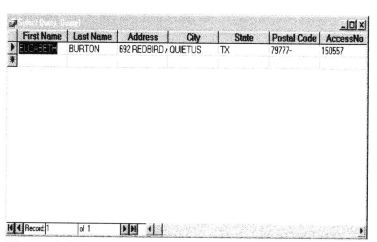

Figure 6.6 Query Results

13.   Save query as April Overdues.

This query, unlike the OVERDUE query, combines the Book table with the LIBUSER table, so information in both tables can be related for informational purposes.

Printing the results we've just seen on the screen is the next step. In chapter 7, we will discuss printing from a query and using reports to design an overdue notice and mailing labels.

CHAPTER 7 REPORTS

OBJECTIVES

7.1 PRINTING FROM THE DATABASE

7.2 REPORT PRINTING

7.3 MAILING LABELS

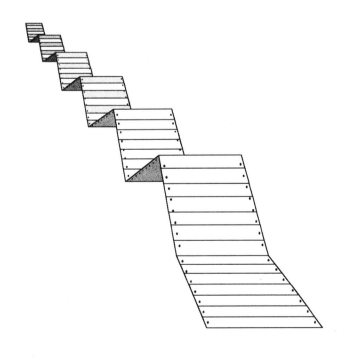

You have learned most of what you need to use
Microsoft Access for Windows:

● how to create a file
● how to add, edit, and delete data
● how to use filters to determine order of the data
● how to use queries to display the data you want
● how to relate tables to make information more
  useful

The only thing left to learn is how to make printed
reports of your information. In this chapter, you will
learn to print from a query and to use Access's design
function to create and print reports for an overdue notice
and mailing labels. Remember the difference between a
query and a report is that queries are a one time file and
reports are recurring.

7.1 PRINTING FROM DATABASE

1.   Before printing we will create a new query named
      SHELFLIST. This query will include information
      to identify the book inventory in the Library. Open
      the LIBRARY database and Click on **Queries** (see
      Figure 7.1).

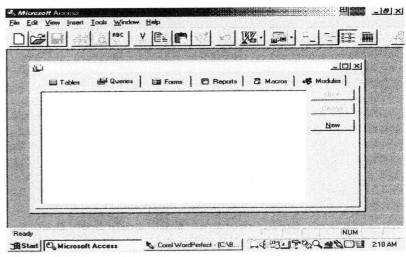

Figure 7.1 Create New Query

2. Click **New**, then click on **Design View** (see Figure 7.2).

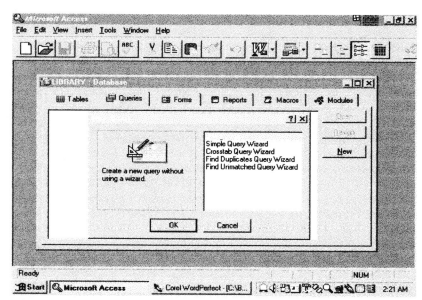

Figure 7.2 New Design View

3. Add the BOOKS table by clicking on **BOOKS** and then on **Add** (see Figure 7.3).

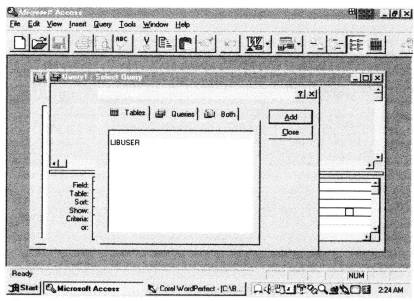

Figure 7.3 Select Tables

4.   **Close** the **Show Tables** dialog box (see Figure 7.4).

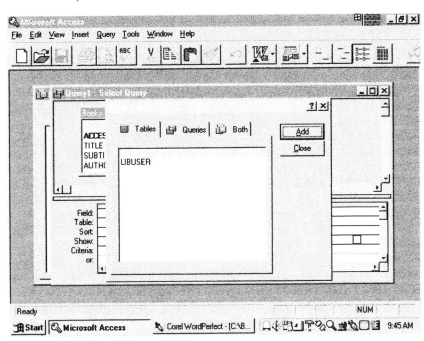

Figure 7.4 Close Show Tables

5.   Select the following fields by double clicking on each: **Title, Author, AccessNo, CallNo,** and **Checkout**.

Paste

6.   Move the **CallNo** field to the first position, so it appears before the Title. Move the cursor above **CallNo;** when the cursor turns into a down arrow, click the mouse then go to the **Edit** menu and click **Cut**. Now, move the cursor above the Title field until the down arrow appears. Go back to the **Edit menu** and click on **Insert Column**. The last step is to **Paste** the **CallNo** information into the blank column by using the **Paste** jar icon (see Figure 7.5).

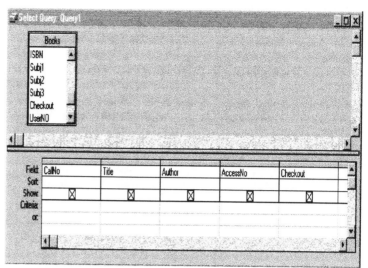

Figure 7.5 Select Query Items

Run

7. **Run** the query (see Figure 7.6).

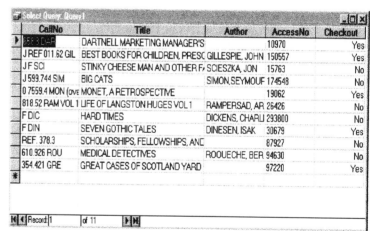

Figure 7.6 Run Query

8. **Save** the query as SHELFLST.

Printer

9. Click on **File** then **Print** or the printer icon.

10. The **Printer Dialog** window appears when print is selected. The top line of the box explains which printer you are using (this should already be set up for you) (see Figure 7.7).

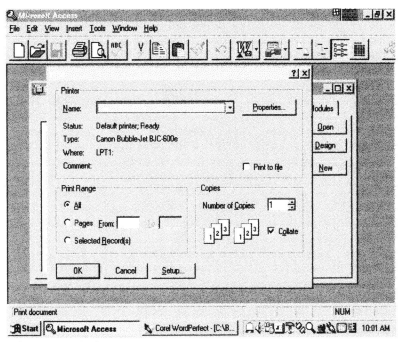

Figure 7.7 Print

11. The **Print Range** box defines exactly what will be
printed:

- **All** will print the entire query.

- **Selected Records** will only print a
highlighted block of information.

- **Pages From** will print a range of pages.

13. **Print Properties** is a window that allows you to
adjust the print quality. The higher the dpi the
better the print quality, but the longer it takes to
print (see Figure 7.8).

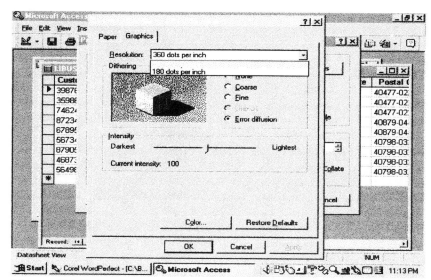

Figure 7.8 Print Properties

14. **Copies** allow you to choose the number of copies that will be printed (1 is the default).

15. **Print to file** means the query will be saved as a print file. This option allows you to print the file later without running Microsoft Access. Choosing this option will bring down a dialog box so you can tell the program where and under what name you want the file saved.

16. Click **OK** and your Shelflist query will print before your eyes.

7.2 REPORT PRINTING

In this section we will learn how to create and print a report of overdue books.

1. Click on **Report** then **New**.

2. This time we will use the **Report Wizard**. Before clicking on that though, fill in the blank for the name of the query we are creating a report from, in this case use APRIL OVERDUE. Now click on the **Report Wizard** (see Figure 7.9).

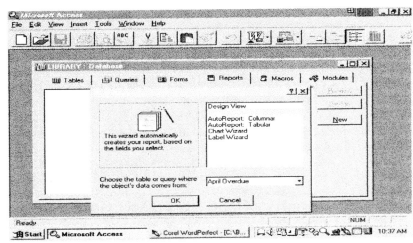

Figure 7.9 Create Report

3.   Double click (in order) the fields to be used in the report. Use the following fields: **FirstName, LastName, Address, City, State, Postal Code, AccessNo, Title, CallNo**, and **DateCheck** (see Figure 7.10).

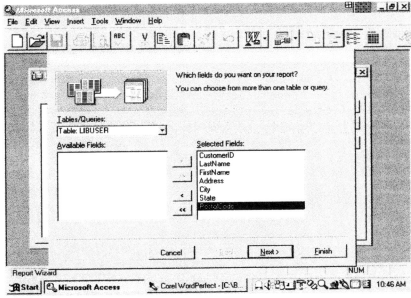

Figure 7.10 Select Table to Use

4. Click on the **Next** button found at the bottom of the **Report Wizard** box. You are asked if you wish to add any grouping levels. Click **Next** (see Figure 7.11).

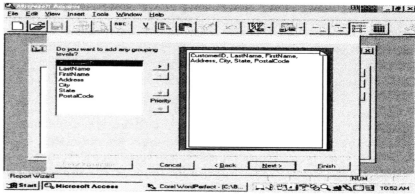

Figure 7.11 Grouping

5. This dialog box is inferring how the data should be sorted, either **ascending** or **decending** order (see Figure 7.12). Double click on the **UserNo** field. Now click **Next**.

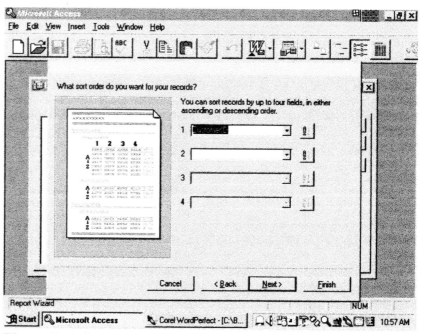

Figure 7.12 Sort Fields

6.   To keep the orientation of the report in Landscape, click **Next** (see Figure 7.13).

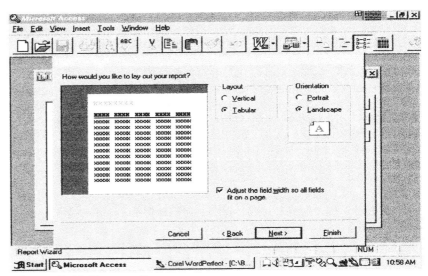

Figure 7.13 Report Layout

7.   Select a style from the selections offered (see Figure 7.14).

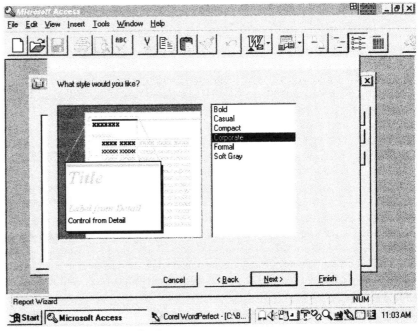

Figure 7.14 Report Style

8.   Title this report OVERDUE BOOK LIST by
     typing the title in the blank available (see Figure
     7.15).

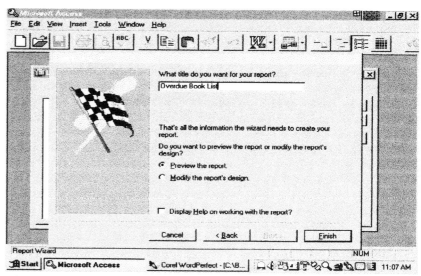

Figure 7.15 Report Title

9.   Click on See all the fields on one page box.

10. Click on **Finish** and the report will appear (see
     Figure 7.16).

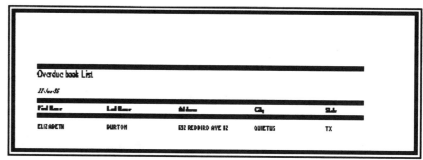

Figure 7.16 Finished Report

Print

11. Now that the report is completed, let's click on the
     Printer button!

12. Click **OK**.

13. **Save** the report as OVERDUE BOOKS.

7.3 Mailing Labels

1. Click **Report,** then **New**, then click on **Label Wizard** (see Figure 7.17).

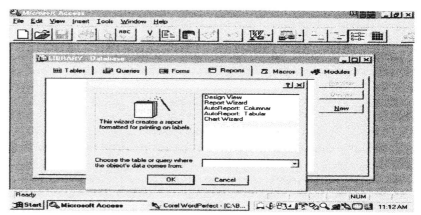

Figure 7.17 Mailing Label Wizard

2. Type in the LibUser table, then click **Report Wizard** (see Figure 7.18).

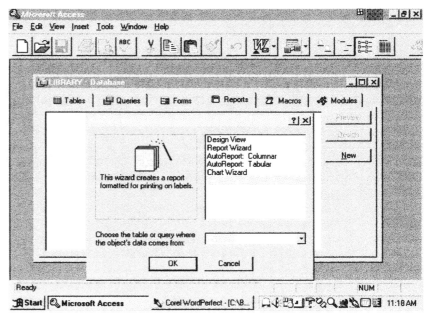

Figure 7.18 Table Selection

3.   Click on **Label Wizard** followed by **OK**. Choose
      the labels (see your book of labels for the number)
      you wish to use and on the following screen, the
      font (see Figure 7.19).

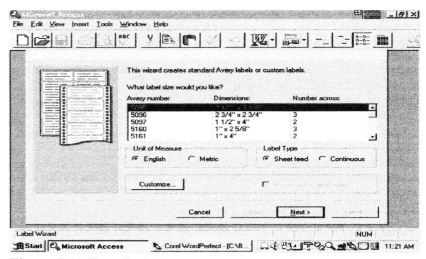

Figure 7.19 Type Label

4.   Click on the fields you would like to use in the

mailing label. Don't forget to add the spaces and
punctuation in the proper place. Below the fields
you will find the punctuation keys. Do **not** use
your keyboard (see Figure 7.20).

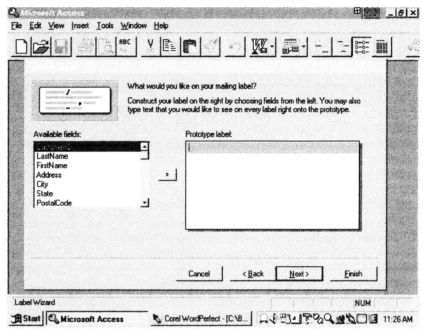

Figure 7.20 Label Fields

5. Type **FirstName** <space>**, LastName**. Click
newline, now type **Address**, click **newline**. Type
City <comma space> State <space> **Postal Code**
(see Figure 7.21).

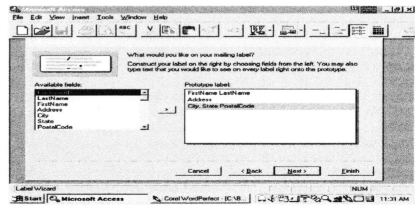

Figure 7.21 Entering Fields

6. Click **Next**.

7. **Sort** by clicking twice on **Postal Code**. Click **Next** (see Figure 7.22).

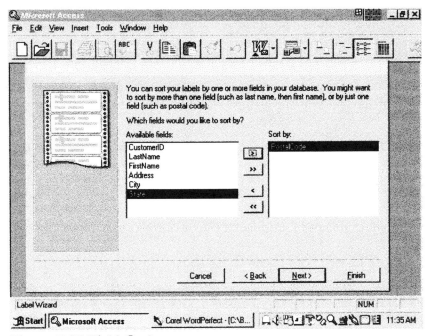

Figure 7.22 Field Order

8. Chose a **Font name, Font size, Font weight**, and **Text color**. In this case we will use the default settings. Click **Finish** (see Figure 7.23).

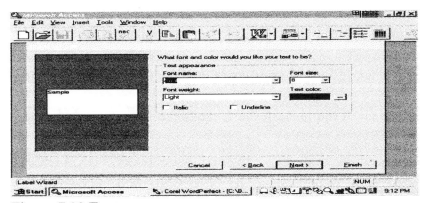

Figure 7.23 Fonts

9. Voila, here is what your labels will look like with the setting you have selected (see Figure 7.24). If this isn't to your liking, it only takes a few minutes to change the settings.

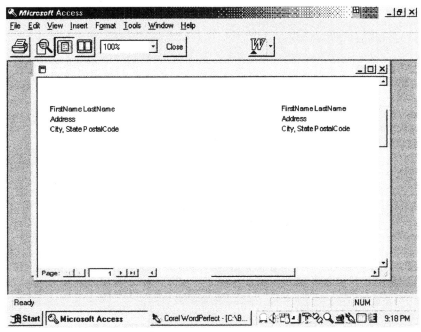

Figure 7.24 Output View

Print

10. **Save** the report as User Mailing List.

11. Click on the **Printer** button, put the labels in your printer and then click **OK**. Watch your mailing labels appear like magic.

GLOSSARY

Access
    A database program produced by Microsoft.

Alphanumeric field
    A location in a record that can contain any combination of letters, numbers, and/or special characters.

Ascend
    An instruction to the system that means ordering data in a field in ASCII order, numbers from smallest to largest, dates from earliest to latest; and letters from A to Z, with upper case and lower case letters considered separate lists.

Data
    Information that is usually in form of alphanumeric characters.

Database
    An organized collection of information; records.

Database Management System
    A software program that facilitates storage, organization, and retrieval of large amounts of related information.

Data entry
    A technique for entering information (data) into a table.

Default

A value or setting that the system or software assumes if no other is specified.

Delete

To remove from the programs; to *remove* a record from the database.

Edit

The process of changing data.

Field

A column in a table; an item of information in a record.

Field type

The kind of information permitted in a specific location in a record. Basic field types include alphanumeric, number, currency ($), date, and logical (Yes / No, True / False.)

Group

A collection of records with at least one similar field.

Index

Reorganizing the order of fields in a table without changing the table structure.

Index field

The designated field(s) that controls the order of records.

Linking tables

Access lets you link tables together to form a relational database, which is, essentially, a database that stores data in multiple tables that you can relate to in useful ways. Linking two tables lets Access draw information from both tables to create forms or answer queries.

Menu

A list of options from which to choose in a computer.

Menu bar

At the top of the screen, divisions that indicate the commands available when using Access during specific times.

Modify

To change a table or data.

Number field

A location in a record that can only contain numbers, a plus or minus sign, and a decimal.

Object

A window element with its own characteristics; it can be moved and sized.

Operator(s)

A feature used to find a range of values rather than an exact match; also called relational operator(s).

Query

A question asked about a table or group of tables.

Record

A row in a table; it contains all the fields for an entity.

Relational Database

A database in which common fields create relationships between tables.

Report form

A designation that determines how information retrieved from the system displays or prints.

Sort

The process of changing the order of the records in a table.

Speed bar

The buttons and tools under the main menu; easy access commands for frequent tasks.

Speed menu

Indicates the options of a screen element.

Table

A database structure in which data are arranged in columns and rows; columns contain fields, and rows contain records; also called a file.

View

A display of a query result.

Wild card(s)

A feature that means "contains" or "includes," substitutes for accuracy.

Index